PRAISE FOR
THE PATIENT'S PRIMARY CARE EXPERIENCE

Piche and Luna's *The Patient's Primary Care* ~~*erful*~~
Partnerships is an informative guide for the ~~mary~~
care clinician, offering strategies to enhance ~~action~~
and to optimize outcomes. It is a must-read primer for any ~~ovider~~
working in the primary care arena.

Donna M. Emanuele, DNP, RN, FNP-BC, ENP-C, CNS, FAANP
Director, Doctor of Nursing Practice Program
College of Graduate Nursing, Western University of Health Sciences

The Patient's Primary Care Experience: A Roadmap to Powerful Partnerships gets it right. It moves beyond patient satisfaction to the experience and, more importantly, patient engagement. This handbook contains just enough theory to lay the foundation for the strategies. The book outlines practical, actionable tools and tips for improving the experience in the ambulatory care setting. The content will help organizations progress from the abstract to the observable.

Nancy DeZellar Walsh, DNP, RN
President and Founder, DeZellar Walsh Consulting, LLC

Primary care is the backbone of the American healthcare system. Piche and Luna provide solid content for maximizing the primary care experience. This book gives providers the strategies, tips, and tools to strengthen the patient-centered medical home through provider and employee engagement. It's a great balance between pragmatic, how-to advice and evidence-based practices. Providers and practice managers will want this as their go-to tool kit, but the ultimate winner is the patient.

Kristin Baird, MHA, BSN, RN
President/CEO, Baird Group
Author, Raising the Bar in Service Excellence

Each of us has had a memorably negative healthcare experience. In this exceptionally valuable volume, the authors present a complete synthesis for a reconstructed, enhanced, ultra-safe, highly satisfying, comprehensive primary care clinic. As you implement these ideas, your clinic will become more rewarding for you and for your patients, and their health will improve. No more bad memories!

G. W. McCarthy, MD, MBA, DAvMed
Hospital CEO, US Air Force, and Veterans Administration

The
Patient's
Primary Care
Experience

A Road Map to Powerful Partnerships

The Patient's Primary Care Experience

A Road Map to Powerful Partnerships

Mary-Ellen Piche | Gina Luna

ACHE Management Series

Library of Congress Cataloging-in-Publication Data

Names: Piche, Mary-Ellen, author. | Luna, Gina, author.
Title: The patient's primary care experience : a road map to powerful partnerships / Mary-Ellen Piche, Gina Luna.
Other titles: Management series (Ann Arbor, Mich.)
Description: Chicago, IL : Health Administration Press, [2022] | Series: ACHE management series | Includes bibliographical references and index. | Summary: "This book makes a business case for improving the patient experience in the primary care setting and presents proven strategies, tools, and templates for enhancing both the patient and staff experience"—Provided by publisher.
Identifiers: LCCN 2021047196 (print) | LCCN 2021047197 (ebook) | ISBN 9781640553323 (paperback : alk. paper) | ISBN 9781640553293 (epub)
Subjects: MESH: Patient-Centered Care | Professional-Patient Relations
Classification: LCC R727.3 (print) | LCC R727.3 (ebook) | NLM W 84.7 | DDC 610.69/6—dc23
LC record available at https://lccn.loc.gov/2021047196
LC ebook record available at https://lccn.loc.gov/2021047197

The paper used in this publication meets the minimum requirements of American National Standard for Information Sciences—Permanence of Paper for Printed Library Materials, ANSI Z39.48-1984. ⊚™

Acquisitions editor: Jennette McClain; Manuscript editor: James Fraleigh; Project manager: Andrew Baumann; Layout: Integra

Found an error or a typo? We want to know! Please e-mail it to hapbooks@ache.org, mentioning the book's title and putting "Book Error" in the subject line.

For photocopying and copyright information, please contact Copyright Clearance Center at www.copyright.com or at (978) 750-8400.

Health Administration Press
A division of the Foundation of the American
   College of Healthcare Executives
300 S. Riverside Plaza, Suite 1900
Chicago, IL 60606-6698
(312) 424-2800

Contents

Foreword

FOR THE PAST four decades, healthcare has struggled to create a system of care delivery that balances quality, safety, and patient-centeredness. Although significant progress has been made on the quality and safety fronts, person- and patient-centered approaches to care have remained aspirational in many settings. The challenge of partnering with patients and families and the fragility of the progress made became frighteningly evident during the COVID-19 pandemic. As safety practices ratcheted up, we saw erosion in most person-centered practices across all settings of care. Out of an "abundance of caution," patients and families were once again marginalized as clinical care teams prioritized risk reduction over the patient experience of care. The consequences of policies enacted with little to no input from the patients and families they were intended to keep safe created unintended and avoidable harm. Once again, the challenge of balancing essential elements of optimal care went unmet.

If we can take one thing away from this recent crisis, it is the importance of creating a more robust, standardized, and enduring patient-centered medical home to achieve that needed balance. As the backbone of our care delivery system, primary care sets the tone and the expectation around the partnership between patients, their families, and members of the care team. Designing a welcoming healing environment that supports the active engagement of all stakeholders can be accomplished with the right roadmap. Mary-Ellen provides that roadmap, focusing on practical tools, tips, and strategies for creating and sustaining an optimal patient experience in primary care settings. In my years of working with Mary-Ellen on implementing the Planetree Patient-Centered Care Model in scores of hospitals and clinics, I was repeatedly impressed by her ability to find concrete methods for achieving aspirational results. The handbook she and Gina Luna have developed shares that knowledge and should be required reading for every primary care practice with a commitment not only to their patients, families, and caregivers, but also to the practice of safe, high-quality, *compassionate* care.

Susan Frampton
President, Planetree International
Author, Putting Patients First: Best Practices in Patient-Centered Care

Preface

HAVE YOU EVER had a "wow!" experience at your primary care visit? An encounter in which you felt fully engaged, heard, and an equal partner in your healthcare? Probably not. Too often we experience delays in getting an appointment, long waiting times after we arrive at the scheduled time, harried staff, and providers who interrupt seconds into our explanation of our reason for the visit.

How do we ensure a consistently positive experience for our patients, every encounter, every time? This book will provide tips and tools to help you on that journey. Make no mistake, this is not a silver bullet. It takes commitment, hard work, and every staff member's connection to purpose.

We have designed, tested, and refined these strategies since 2002 in the primary care setting: specifically, a group of clinics across the country located in both urban and rural areas. As healthcare evolves to meet rapidly changing expectations and a new normal as a result of the COVID-19 pandemic, so must our approaches to providing a fulfilling primary care experience.

CHAPTER CONTENTS AND FEATURES

Chapter 1 lays out the drivers for improving the patient experience in the primary care space. Chapters 2 and 3 explore the key elements of the patient-centered medical home model, including shared medical appointments and telehealth.

Chapters 4 and 5 describe tactics to promote staff and provider engagement by focusing on behavioral standards, reward and recognition, and creating joy in the workplace. Chapter 6 shifts to patient and family engagement, featuring the importance of the social determinants of health and patient activation in creating an effective provider–patient partnership.

Chapter 7 highlights the key aspects of environmental design, including the onstage–offstage model for team-based care. Chapters 8 and 9 focus on measurement—the key performance indicators to evaluate the performance of your primary care practice.

Chapter 10 discusses lessons learned from the COVID-19 pandemic as they apply to the primary care space.

APPENDIX AND RESOURCE LIST

Last, we share several of the tools and templates we have developed and tested such as a shared medical appointment guide, the SMART goal patient worksheet, and a template for showcasing process improvements.

We hope that this material helps all who provide primary care—medical and behavioral health clinicians, nurses, administrators, technologists, social workers, and nutritionists—to deliver the best and safest experience possible for the primary care patient.

CHAPTER 1

The Evolving Landscape of Primary Care

THE UNITED STATES' life expectancy ranking continues to decline, despite its spending far more on healthcare than any other country. The United Nations Population Division (2021) reports the United States has dropped to 46th place, with 79.11 years as the estimate for both sexes combined. At the same time, competition for healthcare services abounds while customers and stakeholders expectations escalate, causing these services to move out of the traditional bricks and mortar and into homes (via phones, computers, health monitors, etc.) and the retail space. New delivery models are also emerging that center the patient in the healthcare practice.

This chapter will explore the factors driving improvement of the patient experience in the primary care space, in light of growing consumer expectations and accreditation requirements and a changing regulatory environment. First let's examine the critical forces shaping the future of primary care delivery.

CONSUMER EXPECTATIONS

The Beryl Institute (2010) defines the patient experience as "the sum of all interactions shaped by an organization's culture that influence patient perceptions across the continuum of care." The first step in this experience is deciding upon a healthcare provider—and today our patients have many choices. They get their information from family, friends and neighbors, social media, news outlets, Medicare's Hospital Compare website, and advertising.

What characteristics set one healthcare organization apart from others? The following domains speak directly to Beryl's "patient perceptions across the continuum."

Access

Access covers the ease of getting an appointment and navigating the healthcare facility, and how long one waits to be seen. High-performing organizations develop smooth, efficient processes to provide a seamless experience. They routinely seek feedback from their patients to continually improve their processes and meet ever-evolving expectations.

Relationships

Patient feedback tells us that relationships are important to their experience. Are patients treated with dignity and respect by the scheduler, the receptionist, and all members of the primary care team (nurse, provider, social worker, pharmacist, nutritionist, etc.)? Are they considered partners in receiving care, setting health goals, and making decisions? We need to listen more and talk less.

The foundation of these relationships is trust, which must be nurtured and built over all touchpoints across the continuum. One negative encounter can erode trust very quickly—it can take as many as three positive encounters to restore the patient–provider relationship. For our patients, trusting relationships are about the emotions generated, their perceptions, and what they remember. How do we make them feel? Are we honest and transparent?

Exhibit 1.1 is a consumer survey by the Beryl Institute that reinforces the relational nature of healthcare. Beryl asked patients the importance of specific aspects of their healthcare experience: communication, competence, the environment and access. As you can see, respondents rated all of these aspects as high.

Safety

Although the exact phrase "First, do no harm" does not appear in the original version (AD 245) of the Hippocratic Oath, keeping patients safe was clearly intended. Fast-forward to the present day with this updated maxim: "zero preventable harm," a call to action for the movement toward high reliability in healthcare. Getting to zero is a journey, and many organizations are transforming the way they work to reach this goal. We will further detail what this means to staff and patients in chapters 4 and 6.

Quality

This domain is characterized by care that is safe, effective, patient centered, timely, efficient, and equitable. In the past our patients might have taken for

Exhibit 1.1: Beryl Institute Consumer Survey

Item	% Rating Item Very or Extremely Important
Listen to you	95
Communicate clearly in a way you can understand	95
Give you confidence in their abilities	94
Take your pain seriously	93
A healthcare environment that is clean and comfortable	94
Provide a clear plan of care and why they are doing it	93
Ask questions and try to understand your needs and preferences	92
The ability to schedule an appointment or procedure within a reasonable time	93
A discharge/check-out process in which your treatment plan and/or next steps in care are clearly explained	92

Source: Adapted from Beryl Institute (2018).

granted that care would be technically sound. They trusted that their providers were qualified, competent, and proficient. Today, Healthcare Effectiveness Data and Information Set measures, satisfaction surveys, Hospital Compare ratings, and accreditation status reports give them the information they need to make informed choices. Providing best-in-class care gives a healthcare organization a competitive edge.

Value

Consumers want to know they are getting the most for their healthcare dollar. The patient investment continues to increase through insurance premiums, copays and, all too often, surprise billing.

But healthcare value goes beyond controlling costs, to medical necessity. Do our patients receive the right treatment, at the right time, in the right setting? High-value care is that which is the highest quality at the lowest possible cost, which conserves our resources to provide better access and equity.

Let's not forget about generational differences. With each new generation, the consumer profile shifts and expands. For instance, baby boomers value their time and money. They seek a primary care provider that offers not only routine exams, but also diagnostic tests and additional services in one location. They tend to be more brand loyal than younger generations and place a premium on reputation.

The Institute of Healthcare Improvement (IHI 2020) maintains that baby boomers need a healthcare system that is "age-friendly, one that aims to cause no harm, uses evidence-based practices and aligns with what matters most to the older adult and their family caregivers" (p. 4). Such a groundbreaking organization offers this framework:

- **What Matters:** Partner with the patient to identify and align care with health outcome goals and preferences.
- **Medication:** Prescribe medication, when needed, that does not interfere with what matters: mentation and mobility.
- **Mentation:** Manage depression, dementia, and delirium.
- **Mobility:** Move safely every day to maintain function and the ability to do What Matters.

Generation Xers use information sources more often than boomers or millennials to make decisions about their healthcare providers. They value convenient access, appreciating walk-in services in the retail setting, both after hours and during the weekend.

> Understanding this wide range of expectations and creating services to address them are key to success in this dynamic environment.

Millennials, also known as Generation Y, value personal relationships to the extent that they will switch providers after a single negative experience. They expect information to be easily accessible and use it to compare healthcare plans and services. Online tools, video visits, and a social media presence will resonate with members of this age group. Understanding this wide range of expectations and creating services to address them are key to success in this dynamic environment.

HEALTHCARE POLICY: VALUE-BASED PAYMENT

The Affordable Care Act (ACA) of 2010 attempted to lay the groundwork for moving from volume to value. Consumers and payers alike, then and now, continue to demand lower-cost options. The short-term focus of the ACA was on testing new payment models linked to quality, cost savings, and infrastructure. Provider reimbursement strategies were aligned with improving clinical process measures/outcomes and patient satisfaction while reducing costs. Through the 2010s, several models were designed and tested: alternative payment models such as accountable care organizations, Comprehensive Primary Care payment, bundled payments, and Medicare's Shared Savings Program.

Population-based models provide coordination of healthcare services (primary care, prevention, chronic care) for the small percentage of the population that use the most resources. We will discuss the concept of population health management in chapter 6.

In the early 2020s we saw some progress in the shift to payment for value. A growing number of payers have moved to this model from fee-for-service payment. More providers are engaged in some form of quality-linked payment; others are experimenting with advanced models focused on population management, which has transformed their practices. Many organizations are reporting that their value-based care models (e.g., care coordination, patient tracking, telehealth) have helped them manage the challenges of the COVID-19 pandemic. They were able to focus on managing their patients with chronic conditions rather than generating revenue to survive.

> Many organizations are reporting that their value-based care models have helped them manage the challenges of the pandemic.

Yet much work needs to be done, as healthcare costs continue to trend upward, healthcare outcomes place the United States in a comparatively low rank against other countries, and disparities along racial and socioeconomic lines continue.

Successful value-based-payment transition takes time. Ongoing experimentation with various models will inform its future. For now, it makes sense to design our primary care services with quality, value, and equitable access in mind.

HEALTH EQUITY

The question of health equity has also been an important one for value-based care. Organizations can only get the best clinical outcomes and fulfill their value-based care contracts when they ensure all patients have the same opportunity to obtain and maintain health.

Topping the Emergency Care Research Institute's (2021) list of the top ten patient safety concerns are racial and ethnic disparities in healthcare. Disparities are seen in the differences in disease screening, severity, complications, and mortality between populations. Race, ethnicity, gender, sexual orientation, and socioeconomic status affect the quality and quantity of healthcare services accessed.

> An inclusive environment ensures equitable access to healthcare resources for all.

An inclusive environment ensures equitable access to healthcare resources for all, and enables individuals and groups to feel safe, respected, engaged, motivated, and valued for who they are.

Disparate treatment, long a barrier for many minority and lower-income patients, has only been exacerbated during the COVID-19 pandemic. Access to testing, vaccines, and treatment has been a challenge for these vulnerable populations. As a result, equity and inclusion have emerged as major national priorities.

What is being done to level the playing field? Many healthcare organizations are being intentional about identifying the impact of the social determinants of health on access to care and are designing creative approaches to ensure that all populations are considered. We will discuss this aspect further in chapter 6.

Here are but a few of the initiatives underway to address health equity and access across the country:

- Researching the connection between poverty and primary care delivery models, care-coordination models, and relationship-based models
- Appointing case managers for vulnerable Medicaid patients
- Establishing community-based care and outreach to bring services closer to vulnerable populations (e.g., sending nurses and EMTs to visit patients who frequently show up in the emergency department)
- Providing staff training and tools related to unconscious bias
- Collecting health equity data and targeting solutions to address gaps
- Instituting more ethical billing practices and price transparency
- Undertaking specific strategies to address the social determinants of health
- Creating chief inclusion and diversity officer positions in large healthcare systems
- Investing recruitment resources and efforts to ensure healthcare providers mirror the populations that they serve (e.g., expanding reach beyond the usual networks to women's associations and ethnic groups, using stratified demographic data to recruit staff and develop cultural competencies).
- Diversifying the supplier base by engaging with women and minority-owned small businesses

How is your organization doing on the equity front? The Institute for Healthcare Improvement (2020; Wyatt et al. 2016) provides a framework and a self-assessment tool to help gauge your performance and focus future efforts:

- Make health equity a strategic priority.
- Develop structure and processes to support health equity work.
- Develop strategies to address the determinants of health.

- Decrease institutional racism.
- Develop community partnerships to improve health and equity.

Here is a simple set of questions to ask about your primary care services:

- Who is benefiting?
- Who isn't benefiting?
- What are the barriers?

Identifying and addressing your organization's needs and the gaps will put it on the path to equitable access. How will you measure your progress? Disaggregating health outcomes data, such as mortality and life expectancy, and process measures (preventative care, treatment of chronic conditions) by ethnicity, race, gender, and socioeconomic status will show where you are closing gaps and point to where more work needs to be done.

The pandemic has been a catalyst for change and innovation with many services shifting to the virtual environment, such as nurse and provider visits or follow-ups for acute and chronic conditions. The digital divide has become another challenge as a barrier for those who do not have a computer or internet access. How do we turn the digital divide into the digital door?

The Joint Commission and Kaiser Permanente have partnered to recognize improvements in healthcare disparities by creating the Bernard J. Tyson National Award for Excellence in Pursuing Healthcare Equity. Tyson, the late chair and CEO of Kaiser Permanente, worked diligently to address equity. This award will highlight measurable and sustained reductions in one or more healthcare disparities.

Now that we have set the stage, let's explore how one specific model of healthcare delivery is addressing these critical issues.

THE EVIDENCE FOR THE PATIENT-CENTERED MEDICAL HOME

As described by the National Committee for Quality Assurance (NCQA 2021), the patient-centered medical home (PCMH), also known as the primary care medical home, is designed to reduce fragmentation and improve quality. The model emphasizes team-based care, communication, and coordination, which have been shown to lead to better care. Higher rates of fragmentation are associated with greater costs, lower quality, and more preventable hospitalizations.

Many payers acknowledge PCMH as a hallmark of high-quality care. It means an organization is providing patient-centered care that is associated with better outcomes; greater patient satisfaction; and a reduction in avoidable, costly visits to the emergency department and hospital. As a result, many payers provide incentives to organizations using this model. In addition, PCMHs are associated with better staff satisfaction. As reported by NCQA, one analysis found implementation of PCMH to increase work satisfaction, whereas reported staff burnout decreased by more than 20 percent (Pines et al. 2015).

The PCMH is a model that puts the patient at the center, at the forefront. Traditionally, our healthcare systems have been designed with the providers and staff in mind, for the organization's convenience rather than the patient's. PCMH turns that on its head—and it's about time. A PCMH gathers a team of people committed to improving the health and healing of individuals in a community. The team embraces patients, families, care partners, and the community in codesigning and coproducing care. It replaces episodic care with a focus on the whole health of the individual.

At its core, the PCMH team typically includes the provider, a nurse, and a medical assistant. Around this core is a circle that includes clinical pharmacists, nutritionists, behavioral health staff, and others, so that in a primary care setting the PCMH can bring together a variety of services for the patient, including telehealth and diagnostics. This all takes place in a healing environment purposefully designed to promote well-being.

The PCMH also has been shown to better manage patients' chronic conditions, such as diabetes. NCQA (2021) reports a Hartford Foundation study that found that 83 percent of patients surveyed reported improved health (Langston, Undem, and Dorr 2014). One pilot program showed a 9.3 percent reduction in ED utilization, resulting in approximately $5 million in annual savings and a 10.3 percent reduction in ambulatory-care-sensitive inpatient admissions for patients with two or more comorbidities (Harbrecht and Latts 2012). Another study reported by NCQA (2021) found PCMH was associated with $265 lower average total Medicare spend per beneficiary, lower hospital spending, and, again, fewer ED visits (Raskas et al. 2012). See additional evidence in exhibit 1.2.

Exhibit 1.2: Evidence to Support Patient-Centered Medical Homes

4.2%–8.3% patients were better on hemoglobin A1c (HbA1c) testing

4.3%–8.5% were better on low-density-lipoprotein cholesterol testing

15.5%–21.5% were better on nephropathy monitoring

9.7%–15.5% were better with eye examinations

Source: Data from Friedberg et al. (2015).

Exhibit 1.3: Impact of Integrated Primary Care on Specific Aspects of Care

Practice	Baseline (2010)	Improvement (2020)
Depression screening	24%	46%
Diabetes care bundle	19.5%	24.6%
Documentation of self-care plans	8.7%	19.5%
Rate of healthcare utilization in visits	23.5%	18.1%

Source: Data from Allen (2020).

Many organizations are taking the next step and integrating mental health into the PCMH with impressive results (exhibit 1.3). Intermountain Healthcare (Allen 2020) routinely provides mental health evaluations and services to all of its primary care patients, which improved healthcare quality and reduced costs by 3 percent. This integrated team-based model of care has produced impressive results across ten years.

LEADERSHIP

How do we meet these challenges? No surprise, the process starts with leadership. The IHI (Balik et al. 2011) identified leadership actions as the first of five primary drivers of exceptional patient experience. Critical to a healthcare organization's success is senior leaders' ability to continually clarify, articulate, and model both the organization's goals for patient and family experience and why they matter. The sequence of patient-centered care deployment matters—leadership comes first!

Transformational leadership displays the following attributes:

- **Promoting a culture of "always versus sometimes":** Be bold, set the bar high, and remain resolute with your convictions and relentless in the quest for excellence. Only the best is good enough for our patients.
- **Patient driven, employee built:** Identify and incorporate patient preferences into the design of healthcare processes and systems while including employees at all stages.
- **Shared vision, shared culture:** Define what success looks like and establish an environment where success can thrive.
- **It's about people, not stuff:** Always display your passion for the mission and purpose, which inspires staff.

Competencies

What are the requisite competencies for a transformational leader? Consider this basic set:

- **Personal mastery:** Making the time to improve one's total self and providing an environment where staff can do the same. It's about balancing professional and personal pursuits. Leaders who are strong in this competency hold a personal vision in line with the organizational vision. They promote and manage change while building resiliency for themselves, their staff, and the organization. They model the organization's behavioral standards, coaching and correcting others continuously.
- **Systems thinking:** Cascading the vision through the organization, connecting the dots (resources, ideas, and people). Uses the latest improvement methods and tools to create efficient systems for maximizing resources. Effective system thinkers never lose sight of the interdependencies of all improvement work while linking strategy to outcomes. I call this "hovering at 30,000 feet" to view how it all fits together and facilitate the integration.
- **Organizational stewardship:** Holding self and others accountable for expected behaviors and deliverables. The leader grows low and middle performers and recruits high performers. Always performing nonjudgmentally, this leader shows appreciation for other's contributions. Stewardship is demonstrated by creating a nurturing environment for growth and development, while acting as a champion for the patient experience.
- **Technical:** Aiming for excellence in all endeavors and driving meaningful outcomes. Effective leaders research approaches, models, and options, synthesizing information into prompt decision making. Additional technical aspects include strategic budget development/execution, managing data and information technology, and creating best-in-class quality indicators.
- **Customer service:** Continually seeking out opportunities to redefine what it means to be extraordinary. The leader focuses on all customers, internal and external, and serves them passionately. Listening posts, focus groups, surveys, and committee representation are just a few examples of how the leader welcomes the customer's voice.
- **Interpersonal effectiveness:** Being authentic, humble, and vulnerable. This can be challenging when leaders are traditionally viewed as strong and near perfect. The new leader listens and learns from all, constantly building

relationships, valuing collaboration, and seeking inspiration from others. Sharing skills, talents, and passions across boundaries, the leader rewards and recognizes those behaviors that align with the organization's values, negotiating to achieve a win-win outcome.

- **Flexibility/adaptability:** Creating change through proactive and visionary leadership. The leader anticipates change—indeed, transformation—by preparing teams for new paradigms while importing strong practices. This skill was certainly put to the test during the COVID-19 pandemic. Additional attributes of this skill include exuding positive energy and honoring separate realities, all while being nimble, agile, and proactive.
- **Creative thinking:** Creating organizational culture with daily actions. Creativity comes from a place of exploring curiosity while seeking cognitive diversity. Generational differences, educational and skill variations, and social and cultural diversity are all valued. The leader encourages "big picture" thinking to create a drive for innovation.
- **Humility:** Appreciating the strengths of others, sharing power, and providing feedback. The leader is not afraid to fail while demonstrating authenticity on the front lines. Constructive feedback is a two-way process with staff and stakeholders.

Informal polls of staff tell us that they value leaders who are decisive yet wise, consistent, and honest; who act with integrity and kindness, admit mistakes, and have the ability to say "I don't know."

In sum, the leader's job in this evolving environment is not to think big, it's to think bigger! Engaging the best people, building vibrant cultures, making good choices, and focusing relentlessly on making a difference for patients and families—it's a tall order! All leaders need to find their True North. As Marcus Aurelius advised, "Keep your principles with you at all times."

> The leader's job in this evolving environment is not to think big, it's to think bigger!

Followership

A transformational leader in partnership with engaged followers makes for a winning formula. All too often we focus on the role of leadership; however, both components are equally important.

> A transformational leader in partnership with engaged followers makes for a winning formula.

What is followership? It's the ability to connect with purpose, align with the strategic direction of an organization, participate fully as a team member, and get results. McCallum (2013) suggests that followers possess these qualities:

- **Judgment:** Knowing when a direction is ethical and appropriate
- **Work ethic:** Believing that good effort is its own reward
- **Competence:** Having the skills to do the job at hand
- **Honesty:** Understanding and executing on the responsibility to speak up
- **Courage:** Speaking up about concerns even in difficult situations
- **Discretion:** Respecting the need to protect information
- **Loyalty:** Acting as a steward of the organization
- **Ego management:** Being a team player with good interpersonal skills

Good followers are engaged high performers who take ownership of the work that needs to be done. They see their role as essential to the organization's success. Many go on to be strong leaders. More on this in chapter 4.

Culture

Leaders build culture. We have all heard the statement, "Culture eats strategy for lunch." The best-laid plans go awry if there isn't a healthy, dynamic culture in which to implement them.

Let's start with defining culture and what it means. It represents all an organization says it is, including its values and people. Culture is exemplified by the stories its leaders, staff, and community tell about the organization. It plays out in what leaders reinforce as important, the expectations they place on behaviors and performance. It encapsulates all that is done, not just directly for patients, but also in building highly engaged work environments.

The holy grail is creating a culture of ownership whereby staff own the mission through connection to purpose. When that happens, accountability follows. We will discuss this concept in detail in chapter 4.

Consider the following keys to a caring culture:

- **Promoting an overarching purpose:** Success is evident when you can ask any staff member why the organization exists, and the response is, "To care for patients."
- **Engaging and empowering staff:** Not just giving them the resources and tools to get the job done, but creating a reflective, learning environment for improvement, and empowering staff to feel that they have the ability to make a difference in the life of a patient.

- **Focusing on personal relationships:** Soft skills are critical. Healthcare is about human beings caring for human beings.
- **Creating a universal language of caring:** How do we talk about the work that we do? Putting the patient and the family at the center changes the dialogue.
- **Removing barriers:** Set expectations, provide support, smooth out variation, remove waste, and get out of the way. Your staff will get the job done.
- **Sharing stories:** Generate your own good news. Put a patient's face on the work through storytelling. Better yet, invite patients to tell their stories at town halls and staff meetings. Create opportunities to make those human connections.

Exhibit 1.4 illustrates the shifts in culture needed to support the dynamics of healthcare change.

Make no mistake: Culture creation is hard work that can take as long as two to five years in a complex organization. This is something leaders cannot leave to chance. It requires focus, intention, and commitment so that it can sustain turnover in leadership teams.

Such an intentional culture starts with defining who you want to be as an organization. There needs to be a strong framework for decision making and a value system that's proactively built from within. The single most challenging barrier to improving the patient experience is cultural resistance.

> The single most challenging barrier to improving the patient experience is cultural resistance.

Positive intentional cultures look like this:

- Caring for, being interested in, and maintaining responsibility for colleagues as friends
- Providing support for one another, including offering kindness and compassion when others are struggling
- Avoiding blame and forgiving mistakes

Exhibit 1.4: Transformational Approaches

Old Way of Doing Business	Transformational Approach
Hierarchical	Empowerment
Lack of urgency	Anticipation of needs
I assume	I ask
The way it is	The way it could be
Silos	Teamwork
Entity focused	Patient focused

- Inspiring one another at work
- Emphasizing the meaningfulness of the work
- Treating one another with respect, gratitude, trust, and integrity

On the flip side are incivility, bullying, lateral violence, passive aggression, and disengagement. I can size up a healthcare organization's culture fairly quickly on my first visit. Does staff make eye contact with me and give me a warm greeting? If I look lost, does someone offer to help me? Do I feel welcome? It's the intangibles that give signals about an organization's culture.

How do you approach this work? Let's look at a model for change management.

CHANGE MANAGEMENT

The pace of change in healthcare requires organizations to manage change for successful innovation and process improvement. All of the attributes listed in the "Competencies" section come into play here, especially flexibility and adaptability—agility is crucial. Systems thinking is evident in organizations that have adopted a strong framework for change management.

The pace of change in healthcare requires organizations to manage change for successful innovation and process improvement.

Sources of resistance to change may include staff being concerned about a loss of control, uncertain about what the change will mean to them or whether they will be successful in this new model. They also may see the change as more work for them. Leaders should identify and enlist as sponsors those who are willing and able to facilitate the change.

Sponsors

Change agents, opinion leaders, and the organization's informal leaders are positioned to lead change. They can be found at all levels: executive, supervisory, and frontline. How do we maximize each of these groups as sponsors for effective change? Consider their roles as seen in Exhibit 1.5.

Assessing the readiness of each potential sponsor for the specific change being undertaken is important. Identify resistance or barriers early and respond with mitigation strategies to ensure a smooth rollout of new ideas and initiatives.

Getting Ready

One of the first steps is to get the organization ready for the change. Preparing discussion points for all sponsors to communicate the "why" will put out a consistent

Exhibit 1.5: Roles and Responsibilities for Change Management

Role	Responsibilities
Executives	Set the vision and the priority for the change. Communicate the "why" of the change. Describe what success looks like with the change. Align strategies and resources. Visibly demonstrate the change behaviors.
Champions	Create awareness for the change. Lead specific change activities: training, design, and implementation teams. Build partnerships for the change with midlevel management and the front line. Visibly demonstrate the change behaviors.
Supervisors	Implement the change practices within their departments. Communicate the change to their staff. Visibly demonstrate the change behaviors.
Frontline staff	Lead a change team at the unit level. Participate in change teams across departments. Visibly demonstrate the change behaviors.

message. It's important for staff to know why the change is happening; what will be different as a result; the risk of not changing; and why is it important to them, your patients, and the community. Appeal to their head and their heart, always connecting to the mission.

Give Them the Tools

Two sets of competencies are critical for a successful transition. First are those that sponsors will need to lead staff through change:

- **Adaptability:** Understanding the "why" and making a personal choice to support the change
- **Creating awareness:** Communicating the "why," connecting it to the broader vision, demonstrating personal support, encouraging dialogue
- **Managing the transition:** Identifying areas of resistance, providing a safe environment for discussion, building staff skills
- **Reinforcing and celebrating success:** Public recognition of contributions and achievements, holding staff accountable for compliance with the change

Next are the competencies and behaviors to support new processes that are part of the change effort. Clearly identify and plan training and skill-building workshops or labs for these new processes and the specific skills to carry them out. Define and communicate behavioral standards, coach to them, and hold staff accountable for them.

Sustain the Change

When preparing for change, create methods for gathering feedback from staff and patients, auditing compliance with new skills and behaviors and celebrating success. Align these efforts with systems already in place. Creating parallel paths for new initiatives is a sure route to fragmentation and duplication, draining the organization's resources and confusing staff. Unite all strategic efforts into one clear trajectory so that everyone can jump onboard.

ACCREDITATION AS A FRAMEWORK FOR DESIGN

What does it take to deliver a high-performing PCMH? Chapters 2 through 9 detail this discussion, but let's start here by taking a look through the eyes of our accreditors. The Health Resources & Services Administration, Joint Commission, Accreditation Association for Ambulatory Health Care, and NCQA have put forth pathways to PCMH certification and recognition. They share several core tenets that put patients at the forefront of the experience:

- Organizational governance and administration
- Team-based care
- Patient–care team relationship
- Patient rights and choice
- Patient safety
- Health literacy and self-management
- Population-based care
- Coordination of care and care transitions
- Access to care
- Performance measurement and quality improvement

Related standards, criteria, and elements of performance help to guide healthcare organizations through a transformation process to best meet the ever-changing needs of our patients. Let's move on to chapter 2 to learn more about PCMHs.

KEY POINTS

- Consumer healthcare decisions are influenced by factors across the domains of access, relationships, safety, quality, and value.
- Understanding and creating services to address differences in generational expectations is key to success in this dynamic environment.
- Many organizations are reporting that their value-based care models—care coordination, patient tracking, telehealth—have helped them deal with the challenges of the COVID-19 pandemic.
- An inclusive environment ensures equitable access to healthcare resources for all.
- The PCMH model emphasizes team-based care, communication, and coordination, which have been shown to lead to better care.
- The sequence of patient-centered care deployment matters—leadership comes first.
- The leader's job in this evolving environment is not to think big, it's to think bigger!
- Transformational leaders in partnership with engaged followers makes for a winning formula.
- Culture creation is hard work that can take as long as two to five years.
- The single most challenging barrier to improving the patient experience is cultural resistance.
- The pace of change in healthcare requires organizations to manage change for successful innovation and process improvement.

REFERENCES

Allen, R. W. 2020. "Reimagining Ambulatory Care as Key to Population Health." *Frontiers of Health Services Management* 37 (2): 3–10.

Balik, B., J. Conway, L. Zipperer, and J. Watson. 2011. *Achieving an Exceptional Patient and Family Experience of Inpatient Hospital Care.* Cambridge, MA: Institute for Healthcare Improvement.

Beryl Institute. 2018. *Consumer Perspectives on Patient Experience.* Published July. www.theberylinstitute.org/page/PXCONSUMERSTUDY.

———. 2010. *Defining Patient Experience.* Published September. www.theberylinstitute.org/store/ViewProduct.aspx?id=3720810.

Emergency Care Research Institute. 2021. "Top 10 Patient Safety Concerns 2021." Published July. www.ecri.org/top-10-patient-safety-concerns-2021.

Friedberg, M. W., M. B. Rosenthal, R. M. Werner, K. G. Volpp, and E. C. Schneider. 2015. "Effects of a Medical Home and Shared Savings Intervention on Quality and Utilization of Care." *Journal for the American Medical Association Internal Medicine* 175 (8): 1362–68.

Harbrecht, M., and L. Latts. 2012. "Colorado's Patient-Centered Medical Home Pilot Met Numerous Obstacles, Yet Saw Results Such as Reduced Hospital Admissions." *Health Affairs.* Published September. www.healthaffairs.org/doi/10.1377/hlthaff.2012.0359.

Institute for Healthcare Improvement. 2020. *Age-Friendly Health Systems: Guide to Using the 4Ms in the Care of Older Adults.* Published July. www.ihi.org/Engage/Initiatives/Age-Friendly-Health-Systems/Documents/IHIAgeFriendlyHealthSystems_GuidetoUsing4MsCare.pdf.

Langston, C., T. Undem, and D. Dorr. 2014. "Transforming Primary Care: What Medicare Beneficiaries Want and Need from Patient-Centered Medical Homes to Improve Health and Lower Costs." John A. Hartford Foundation. Published July 25. www.johnahartford.org/images/uploads/resources/NCQA-Hartford_Langston_Slides.pdf.

McCallum, J. S. 2013. "Followership: The Other Side of Leadership." *Ivey Business Journal.* Published September/October. https://iveybusinessjournal.com/publication/followership-the-other-side-of-leadership/.

National Committee for Quality Assurance (NCQA). 2021. "Patient-Centered Medical Home (PCMH)." Accessed August 18. www.ncqa.org/programs/health-care-providers-practices/patient-centered-medical-home-pcmh/.

Pines, J. M., V. Keyes, M. van Hasselt, and N. McCall. "Emergency Department and Inpatient Hospital Use by Medicare Beneficiaries in Patient-Centered Medical Homes." *Annals of Emergency Medicine* 65 (6): 652–60.

Raskas, R. S., L. M. Latts, J. R. Hummel, D. Wenners, H. Levine, and S. R. Nussbaum. 2012. "Early Results Show WellPoint's Patient-Centered Medical Home Pilots Have Met Some Goals For Costs, Utilization, and Quality." *Health Affairs.* Published September. www.healthaffairs.org/doi/abs/10.1377/hlthaff.2012.0364.

United Nations Population Division. 2021. "Life Expectancy of the World Population." Published March. www.worldometers.info/demographics/life-expectancy/.

Wyatt, R., M. Laderman, L. Botwinick, K. Mate, and J. Whittington. 2016. *Achieving Health Equity: A Guide for Health Care Organizations.* Cambridge, MA: Institute for Healthcare Improvement.

CHAPTER 2

The Patient-Centered Medical Home

THE PATIENT-CENTERED MEDICAL HOME (PCMH) has transformed the way patient care is delivered by promoting patient well-being and high-quality patient outcomes. This healthcare model revolves around the patient by focusing on building relationships and enhanced communication with them, which leads to better coordination and comprehensiveness. Value-based healthcare is no longer an exception; it has become the expectation.

FIVE CORE ELEMENTS OF THE PCMH

The US Department of Health and Human Services (2020) has identified five core elements of the PCMH:

- Patient-centered care
- Comprehensive care
- Coordinated care
- Accessible services
- Quality and safety

Patient-Centered Care

The concept of patient-centered care focuses on engaging the patient as the primary treatment-plan decision maker while encouraging them to incorporate their values, preferences, needs, and goals into that plan. The primary care team facilitates this process through patient education and interviewing while respecting the patient's wishes, needs, and values. This process creates a collaborative experience for the patient and helps them reach the most appropriate and beneficial decisions.

Patients engaged in this kind of care are more invested in their health goals and feel their emotional and mental needs are also being met. Additionally, from an organizational perspective, patient-centered care increases the likelihood of the patient's buy-in and commitment to improving their health.

Exhibit 2.1 shows the perceived benefits of patient-centered care.

Exhibit 2.1: Benefits of Patient-Centered Care

Patient	Organization
Improved relationship between patient and primary care team	Improvement in quality metrics
Improved communication between patient and primary care team	Increased staff productivity and efficiency
Patient empowerment through decision-making responsibility	Improved patient satisfaction scores
Healthcare tailored to individual needs and wants	Improved allocation of resources
Higher sense of need fulfillment as individual preferences and values are considered	Improved reputation

Comprehensive Care

Comprehensive care expands on standard healthcare delivery to look at the patient's well-being by incorporating mental, emotional, social, and financial needs while assessing their health literacy. By addressing these specific needs, along with their physical needs, higher-quality outcomes are more likely. When patients' full well-being is addressed, they have better odds of staying engaged and committed to reaching their healthcare goals.

Exhibit 2.2 lists examples of services that should be offered to the patient after the primary care team assesses for additional needs. The organization does not need to provide all the services outlined in the table, but it should address patients' need for these services through screening at each visit. The primary care team must be well versed on the services available within the community and provide patients with information and assistance to utilize them.

Once the primary care team has assessed the patient's physical, mental, emotional, social, and financial needs, it should assess the patient's ability to receive, process, and understand their healthcare information. Various assessment tools are

Exhibit 2.2: Services Offered Under Comprehensive Care

Mental	Emotional	Social	Financial
Therapy	Caregiver support	Food resources	Job training
Crisis hotline	Marital counseling	Residential program	
Addiction counseling			

available to the primary care team; to further illustrate this process, we will use the Rapid Estimate of Adult Literacy in Medicine–Short Form (REALM-SF; see exhibit 2.3). The REALM-SF was created by the Agency for Healthcare Research and Quality (AHRQ) to assess what is needed for the patient to make appropriate healthcare decisions. The tool is normally administered by the licensed practical nurse (LPN) during the initial visit and whenever

> An understanding of the patient's ability to process and receive information guides the primary care team in tailoring instructions and patient education.

Exhibit 2.3: Rapid Estimate of Adult Literacy in Medicine–Short Form

Instructions to read to patients:

Providers often use words that patients don't understand. We are looking at words providers often use with their patients to improve communication between healthcare providers and patients. Here is a list of medical words. Starting at the top of the list, please read each word aloud to me. If you don't recognize a word, you can say "pass" and move on to the next word.

Word list to provide to patients:

Behavior	Jaundice
Exercise	Anemia
Menopause	Antibiotics
Rectal	

Scoring:

0: Suggests third grade and below; will not be able to read most low-literacy materials; will need repeated oral instructions, materials composed primarily of illustrations, or audio or video tapes.

1–3: Suggests fourth to sixth grade; will need low-literacy materials, may not be able to read prescription labels.

4–6: Suggests seventh to eighth grade; will struggle with most patient education materials; will not be offended by low-literacy materials.

7: Suggests high school; will be able to read most patient education materials.

Source: Adapted from Agency for Healthcare Research and Quality (2019).

there is a significant change in the patient's health that affects cognitive abilities. An understanding of the patient's ability to process and receive information guides the primary care team in tailoring instructions and patient education.

Now that the patient's mental, emotional, social, and financial needs and health literacy have been assessed, a comprehensive care plan can be formulated with the needed interventions and services in place to increase the odds for patient success. By incorporating these additional components, the primary care team can provide solutions to help overcome barriers, organize needed resources, incorporate interventions, and offer any additional needed support to ensure a more thorough care experience for the patient. Many comprehensive care plans exist, including those created by the Centers for Disease Control and Prevention (2020).

> Keep in mind that effective use of a comprehensive care plan requires that it be reviewed at each patient visit.

Exhibit 2.4 depicts the Comprehensive Care Plan Life Cycle, modified for incorporation into the PCMH.

Keep in mind that effective use of a comprehensive care plan requires that it be reviewed at each patient visit to assess for any new barriers or changes in goals and to ensure needed interventions, resources, and referrals are obtained.

Exhibit 2.4: Modified Comprehensive Care Plan Life Cycle

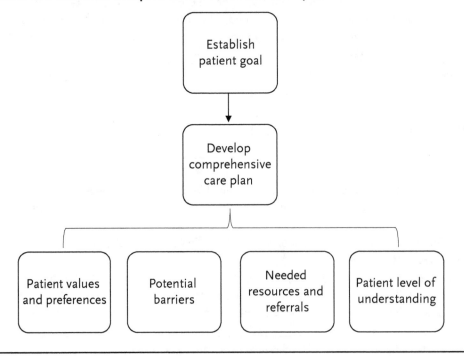

Coordinated Care

Once the primary care team has incorporated the first two elements of the PCMH and has developed a better overall picture of what comprehensive care means for the patient, the execution of care must be coordinated to ensure that all team members and services are utilized to the maximum benefit of the patient's needs. In the PCMH, coordination of care occurs at various levels among primary care, specialty care, hospitals, skilled nursing facilities, and other healthcare systems.

As the case manager, the registered nurse typically oversees coordination, taking on the responsibility for proper communication and transferring essential medical information among members of the primary care team.

A useful tool for organizing and communicating pertinent patient information to achieve coordinated care is the situation, background, assessment, and recommendation (SBAR) form. Advocated by the Institute for Healthcare Improvement (2021), this tool provides essential information about a patient's condition to all members of the primary care team.

A common scenario for a breakdown in communication and lack of coordination in care is when a patient is hospitalized. The SBAR is traditionally used within the hospital setting, but it can also be used by the primary care team to communicate to the hospital team.

Exhibit 2.5 shows the needed components of a successful SBAR when implemented in the primary care setting to communicate with a hospital.

When coordination of care is properly executed, the organization can expect to see greater patient satisfaction, increased patient confidence in the primary care team, and improved utilization management.

When coordination of care is lacking, the organization can experience the following:

- Lack of documentation
- Poor communication
- Missing information
- Delays in care
- Medication errors
- Poor patient outcomes
- Inappropriate and costly utilization of services

Accessible Services

To ensure comprehensive and well-coordinated care, the patient should always have access to the primary care team and the resources necessary to complete the treatment plan. Traditionally access has been available through face-to-face visits.

Exhibit 2.5: Components of a Successful SBAR

Element	Description
Situation	Concise statement of the patient's diagnoses and medication
Background	Pertinent history
Assessment	Status of patient's conditions (controlled vs. uncontrolled)
Recommendation	Requested actions while taking patient's preference into account

With advancements in technology, however, evolving delivery methods have created new nontraditional virtual options for access.

Nontraditional modalities of healthcare access include the following:

- Telephone appointments
- Emails through patient portals
- Telemedicine video appointments
- Shared medical appointments

These forms of nontraditional access eliminate barriers created by geographical distance and time constraints while providing multiple platforms for communication between the patient and primary care team.

Having a multidisciplinary team that is highly skilled in using virtual care also increases patient access by providing multiple opportunities for team member–patient interaction. A multidisciplinary team readily available to the patient improves communication, provides opportunities to assist the patient with overcoming obstacles or barriers, increases patient adherence to the treatment plan, and improves the overall quality of the patient's experience.

As patient needs change, a face-to-face visit may no longer be the most convenient or efficient way to provide care. The organization must evolve to match these needs while eliminating barriers to providing care. Incorporating the preceding nontraditional methods can effectively accomplish this goal.

Exhibit 2.6 explains the benefits of virtual care to the patient and organization.

Access to Shared Medical Appointments

An innovative way to deliver care to many patients at once, while increasing efficiency and utilization of multiple team members, is through shared medical appointments (SMAs). SMAs are group visits that provide an integrated approach to more frequent follow-up care. This type of appointment is well suited for patients requiring chronic disease management such as heart failure, diabetes, hypertension, and chronic obstructive pulmonary disease.

Exhibit 2.6: Benefits of Virtual Care

Patient	Organization
Remove geographical distance—now you can see your provider anywhere.	Removing a geographical barrier creates a larger pool of patients who can be seen.
No need to take time from work.	Cost-effective, less overhead needed than face-to-face visit.
Avoid long wait times in the lobby.	
Be seen from the comfort of home or another location of the patient's choosing.	Higher patient satisfaction rates.
	Better communication as the patient is in a more comfortable setting.
Save on the cost of gas to get to the appointment.	Improved patient outcomes.
	Decrease in missed appointments.
More flexibility and convenience.	

SMAs provide a sense of the patient's "medical home" by facilitating better patient outcomes through a team-based approach to coordinated care, increased access, longer amount of time spent with the primary care team, and a tailored treatment plan focused on the patient's individual needs. They create the opportunity for patients to be seen more frequently and have been shown to increase total quality of care and patient satisfaction. Additionally, SMAs can lessen the need for specialty referral, because the provider is able to see the patient on a more frequent basis, providing opportunities for interventions before patient symptoms decline to the point where referral to a specialist becomes necessary.

Exhibit 2.7 shows the benefits of SMAs to the patient and organization.

Quality and Safety

To ensure patient safety and high-quality care, the healthcare organization must set the standard for using evidence-based practice and implementing best practices

Exhibit 2.7: Benefits of Shared Medical Appointments

Patient	Organization
More time available with primary care team to voice concerns and barriers.	More time to assess barriers and provide interventions.
Relaxed environment with supportive peers who have similar diagnoses and concerns.	Coordination of care with other team members.
Increased education with more opportunities to ask questions.	Increased efficiency through delivering the same message to multiple patients at once.

across all teams. The US Department of Health and Human Services states that healthcare quality comprises the following traits:

- **Safety:** Not simply the absence of adverse or sentinel events, safety focuses on risk reduction and error prevention while providing education and safeguards to support the primary care team.
- **Efficiency:** The appropriate utilization of resources to reduce waste, which can be in the form of cost, resources, or time.
- **Patient-centeredness:** The patient acts as the main decision maker.
- **Timeliness:** Ensuring interventions are activated before harm or unwanted effects can occur. For the primary care team, timeliness can refer to work productivity.
- **Effectiveness:** The impact of an intervention. Every day in healthcare various interventions are trialed to determine what will elicit the best results. Tracking these results leads to best practices and high-quality outcomes.
- **Equitable:** The quality of care does not vary based on the patient.

These aspects of quality and safety must be continuously measured and improved through performance improvement (PI) initiatives. The PCMH supports PI initiatives because of its team-based environment. When establishing PI initiatives, the organization should aim for high impact, high volume. Safety efforts should be focused on decreasing adverse outcomes in high-risk populations and avoiding errors.

Exhibit 2.8 provides examples of performance initiatives focusing on quality and safety that we have instituted in our organization.

Exhibit 2.8: Performance Initiative Examples

Quality and Safety Element	PI Project
Safety	Reducing quantity of high-dose opioids
Efficiency	Ensuring patient lab work is complete before seeing the provider
Patient-centered	Creating SMART goals (discussed in chapter 3) for patients with diabetes
Timeliness	Closing all patient charts within 48 hours
Effectiveness	Provider education on correct usage of antibiotics
Equitable	Screening all patients for food and housing resources

THE PCMH TEAM

A multidisciplinary team-based approach is the key element in effectively implementing the PCMH. This team-based framework, with well-defined roles for each team member, fosters the enhanced collaboration necessary to meet all the patient's needs. Identifying team members as primary and supporting players is the foundation. Once a multidisciplinary team is in place, the patient will have better access to a wider range of services and will be more likely to have their healthcare needs met. With this in mind, the first step in developing the team is defining the primary and supporting roles:

- Provider (physician, nurse practitioner, physician assistant)
- Registered nurse (RN)
- LPN or licensed vocational nurse (LVN)
- Scheduler

Provider

The provider (physician, nurse practitioner, physician assistant) functions as the team leader and guides the patient in the decision-making process. Through effective communication and a focus on what the patient feels is important, the provider partners with and supports the patient in setting goals given the signs and symptoms of the present disease, illness, or patient concern. Providers must take special care to avoid becoming the decision maker and must exercise caution to ensure they are presenting the patient with options rather than predetermined plans. The patient should feel that the provider is only guiding the decision-making process, providing support for the creation of patient goals while supplying the tools needed to achieve them.

Registered Nurse

The RN traditionally functions as a case manager to manage the patient's healthcare experience. RNs are tasked with a critical list of duties, including the following:

- Coordinating and tracking referrals
- Facilitating safe transitions
- Providing education
- Ordering necessary supplies
- Ensuring continuity of care
- Aiding communication with other members of the PCMH team

The RN ensures these tasks are met through frequent communication with the patient and the rest of the primary care team. Regular contact between the RN and the patient provides the opportunity for the patient to ask questions, express changes in goals, and report experiences throughout the episode of care. The RN becomes the critical bridge between the patient and the primary care team. A team that functions without an effective RN is likely to encounter frequent disruptions, delays in care, and ultimately patient dissatisfaction.

Licensed Vocational or Practical Nurse

LVNs and LPNs are critical in shaping the patient's experience through pre-appointment planning and data collection. During pre-appointment planning, these nurses connect with the patient before the appointment to determine their needs, which creates a more efficient and thorough visit for provider and patient. Additionally, pre-appointment planning allows the nurses to determine which type of visit is most beneficial for the patient, a critical step in reducing missed appointments.

A common reason for patients missing an appointment, or a no-show, is their inability to get time off from work. A pre-appointment telephone call to the patient gives the LPN or LVN the opportunity to confirm the appointment and offer a more convenient type of appointment if needed, such as over telephone or video. Imagine offering the patient the convenience of a video appointment during their lunch break, eliminating the need to take time off from work. A missed patient appointment can be detrimental to the patient's health, especially in the primary care setting. Pre-appointment planning drastically lowers this risk.

Scheduler

The scheduler often functions as the first point of contact with the patient through coordinating appointments, selecting the appropriate type of appointment (face to face, video, or telephone), and ensuring appointments occur in the correct sequential order. The scheduler must understand the benefits and limitations of each type of appointment. Knowing what can and cannot be offered to the patient based on the nature of the appointment type helps the scheduler guide the patient in selecting the type that meets the patient's healthcare needs and fits with their lifestyle and daily schedule. The scheduler can also assist with the process of data gathering by obtaining medical records and any needed forms for the appointment.

A PROVIDER'S PERSPECTIVE ON PCMHS

Now that we have presented the primary care team, I (Gina) would like to offer the provider perspective, so let us pause for a moment and transition to the meaningfulness of the PCMH to providers. Early in my career, I worked as a nurse practitioner in a chronic pain management facility. The clinic mainly treated chronic back pain through oral pain meds and back injections.

Every day was met with a high volume of patients who required adjustments in pain medication, pain reassessments, imaging ordering and interpretation, determining appropriateness of interventions, scheduling back injections, and patient education and preparation.

I could easily see up to 50 patients per day with the aid of a medical assistant (MA). Not only was this process exhausting, but it was also fast paced, which affected my ability to ensure thoroughness in the level of care I was providing—which likely affected patient satisfaction.

The MA and I knew we needed a team if we were to continue in this clinic and provide high-quality care. If we had a dedicated RN to provide case management and a scheduler (as much of our time was spent on making patient appointments for procedures), this would have made a difference in the level of care and time we could have provided to the patients. The time we spent on these additional duties was costly to the patient's overall visit. With a dedicated team, I could have focused more on the patient's goals and complete well-being. Instead, I only lasted ten months in this environment and the MA also left.

I left this job for a position in primary care where the PCMH model was being initiated. The MA I had worked with joined me, as she, too, was looking for a team-based environment.

Now let us return to the PCMH and look at the benefits of the supporting players.

SUPPORTING PRIMARY CARE TEAM

The PCMH focuses on treating the patient as a whole. To best do this, the healthcare organization must offer additional services, including mental health, medication management, education, and social services.

The supporting primary care team often comprises the following:

- Nutritionist
- Pharmacist
- Behavioral health staff
- Nurse educator
- Social worker
- Medical assistant

Nutritionist

Many chronic diseases, such as diabetes, heart failure, and kidney disease, are affected by diet. The benefit of incorporating a nutritionist into a patient's plan of care is the ability to tailor a nutrition plan specifically to the disease. For chronic disease management, a nutritionist can help inform the patient which dietary choices can relieve or worsen their illness. They can be a resource and coach for the patient to keep them on track to meeting their healthcare goals.

Pharmacist

Pharmacists are experts at determining medication appropriateness for patients and thus are vital for patient safety. When incorporated into the team, a pharmacist can educate the provider and offer additional options for the patient's medication treatment plan. A pharmacist can improve medication compliance by advising the patient on how to take the medicine correctly and any side effects.

Behavioral Health Staff

Behavioral health staff includes designated social workers, counselors, and mental health providers. This service should be distinguished from mental health as it focuses on patient behaviors and how they affect overall well-being. The main goal for this supportive service focuses on improving patient behaviors to promote a healthier life. Common diagnoses where the application of behavioral health services can be helpful are obesity, diabetes, smoking cessation, and substance abuse disorders.

Nurse Educator

For the purposes of this chapter, *nurse educator* will refer to a nurse who educates both staff and patients. She is key to providing other team members with the guidance and education necessary to enact process improvements. Additionally, the nurse educator can provide the patient with education and support in the development and application of self-management skills.

Social Worker

Social workers provide various kinds of support to patients and their families. From emotional support to financial resources, social workers assist patients with coping mechanisms needed to reach their goals. Social workers can work in such capacities as child welfare, legal rights for individuals with disabilities or substance use disorders, occupational assistance, and patient advocacy to name a few.

Medical Assistant

When well cross-trained, medical assistants can be key utility players who are able to fulfill other roles when needed such as those of schedulers, educators, and LPNs/LVNs.

Now that we have identified the team players, in chapter 3 we will provide the map for creating the strong foundation. This includes a comprehensive orientation with clearly defined roles for each player.

THE PROVIDER'S PERSPECTIVE CONTINUED

Let us look back at how the supporting players in the PCMH, particularly a pharmacist and behavioral health counselor, could have been advantageous during my time at the pain clinic for both me and the patients.

First, we would have benefited from a pharmacist to help tailor the patients' pain medication regimens and ensure they were on safe doses of medication. Sharing this workload with a pharmacist would have afforded me additional time to spend with patients to better assess their pain levels, understand their treatment goals, provide education, and involve patients in their treatment plan.

Second, involving a behavioral health counselor could have empowered these patients with coping techniques and behavioral changes to assist with pain management. This likely would have helped to reduce the amount of pain medication they needed. As a provider, I would have spent less time renewing pain meds and scheduling injections, because patients would have achieved similar pain reduction outcomes through the techniques offered by the behavioral health counselors. Patients would have been happier, and outcomes would have been better.

Without a PCMH team, I was unable to provide comprehensive, patient-centered care. Instead, I came to each patient visit with time constraints and a predetermined plan.

By contrast, at my new job, with a team of dedicated individuals under the PCMH model, I began to have more time to focus on delivering better care tailored to the patient. I was no longer in a self-preservation mode to get through the visit and to the next patient.

Using the PCMH model, I began to flourish. I was able to give the care my patients deserved and that I knew I was capable of. I found that my patient's satisfaction was high, and outcomes were continually improving. I felt fulfilled as a provider.

THE BENEFIT OF THE PCMH DURING A PANDEMIC OR OTHER CRISIS

During the COVID-19 pandemic, the PCMH model has proven to be a necessity for the continuation of healthcare delivery, especially during quarantine and isolation. The PCMH's various modalities for access to care support the need for social distancing while ensuring coordination of care and comprehensiveness. The various telemedicine capabilities provide the patient with a way to connect while maintaining distancing protocols. By using the PCMH, healthcare organizations can continue to provide care during times of crisis and instability.

KEY POINTS

- The PCMH model is essential for innovative healthcare delivery.
- A multidisciplinary team must be created and well equipped to carry out the PCMH model.
- Patient-centered care leads to better patient outcomes and higher patient satisfaction.
- Comprehensive care ensures the whole patient is addressed.
- Coordination ensures the transferring of needed patient information to avoid adverse outcomes.
- Offering various types of access is beneficial to the patient and organization.
- Quality and safety should be continuously measured and improved.
- Resources must be aligned with patient needs.

REFERENCES

Agency for Healthcare Research and Quality. 2019. "Health Literacy Measurement Tools (Revised)." Published November. www.ahrq.gov/health-literacy/index.html.

Centers for Disease Control and Prevention. 2020. "Alzheimer's Disease and Healthy Aging: Develop a Care Plan." www.cdc.gov/aging/develop-care-plan.html.

Institute for Healthcare Improvement. 2021. "SBAR Tool: Situation-Background-Assessment- Recommendation." Accessed September 13. www.ihi.org/resources/Pages/Tools/SBARToolkit.aspx.

US Department of Health and Human Services. 2020. "About Healthcare Quality." https://health.gov/our-work/health-care-quality/about-health-care-quality.

CHAPTER 3

How to Implement the Patient-Centered Medical Home

Now that we have defined the components of the patient-centered medical home (PCMH) in chapter 2, let's dive into how you can implement these components to establish a successful PCMH in the primary care setting.

LAYING THE FOUNDATION

Before beginning the implementation process, the organization must develop the foundation for the PCMH by assembling the primary care team. As detailed in chapter 2, the team consists of four key members: a provider, a registered nurse (RN), licensed practical or vocational nurse (LPN or LVN), and scheduler.

A well-functioning team is critical to successfully implementing the PCMH; thus, training for and orientation to the PCMH should be provided. Training and orientation should address each team member's role within the model, focusing on the role's specific duties and expectations.

During training, a PCMH mentor should perform frequent check-ins to discuss concerns, barriers, and items that need clarification. Exhibit 3.1 details each team member's general roles, which can vary with the implementing organization and team makeup.

Now that you have established the team, you can implement the PCMH in your organization.

Exhibit 3.1: Team Roles

Team Member	Role
Provider (physician, nurse practitioner, or physician assistant)	Patient guide: • Patient education • Encourage questions • Discuss options • Guide decision making
Registered nurse	Case management: • Coordinate care • Ensure needed services are in place • Ensure comprehension of care plans
Licensed vocational/practical nurse	Data collection and pre-appointment planning: • Obtain needed information for appointments • Report patient status to the team
Scheduler	Appointment navigator: • Ensure appropriateness of appointment type • Guarantee timely follow-up

IMPLEMENTING THE FIVE CORE ELEMENTS OF THE PCMH

As described in chapter 2, the PCMH has five core elements:

- Patient-centered care
- Comprehensive care
- Coordinated care
- Accessible services
- Quality and safety

We will now take a closer look at each element, using a fictional patient, Mr. Roberts, as a case study.

Patient-Centered Care Through "SMART" Goals

Patient-centered care must guide the decision-making process. Primary care teams can accomplish this by incorporating patients' values, needs, and preferences in patient goals. Setting patient goals helps guide behaviors to promote well-being and good outcomes.

> **Pearl 1: Start each patient visit by asking, "What is your healthcare goal and how can I help you reach it?"**

Case Study: Mr. Roberts has had uncontrolled diabetes for 20 years compounded by a history of diabetes-related foot ulcers. He has seen various providers without any success in improving his diabetes. Each provider he sees tells him the same thing: "Your A1c is very high. You must take your insulin to control your diabetes." Mr. Roberts continues to be frustrated as he has a fear of needles that he does not think he will ever overcome; thus, he feels defeated and gives up on controlling his diabetes.

Mr. Roberts presents in your office and states he just cannot bring himself to administer his insulin injections. This time, the provider asks, "What is your goal for your healthcare?" Mr. Roberts responds, "I would like to control my diabetes without using insulin." This simple interaction lets the provider know that Mr. Roberts's goal is to control his diabetes and is willing to try a different pathway to achieve this.

> **Pearl 2: Always offer options.**

Rather than reinforcing a previously failed plan (i.e., taking insulin), the provider lays out different options for Mr. Roberts. These include seeing a nutritionist to assist with carbohydrate counting and weight loss, enrolling in shared medical appointments for patients with diabetes to help troubleshoot day-to-day problems, and working with a pharmacist to determine what combination of oral medication will help lower Mr. Roberts's blood sugar level. Mr. Roberts opts to try a combination of taking oral medication and seeing the nutritionist.

The provider's role is to present options and guide the patients in making healthcare decisions that help them achieve their goals. In Mr. Roberts's case, the previous providers wanted him to control his diabetes using insulin. Although they likely followed guidelines and evidence-based practice, injections were not realistic for him and thus not achievable.

Mr. Roberts's experience with the new provider made him feel hopeful that he would be able to control his diabetes, as he was given multiple options to succeed. He was able to actively participate in his care by voicing his concerns, establishing a goal, and partnering with his provider to attain it. Over the next year, with frequent check-ins and communication, he sees his blood sugar level decrease and feels more confident in managing his diabetes.

Patients Should Establish Their Own SMART Goals

Attaining high-quality outcomes depends on how patient goals are established. Goals should be specific, not general. To ensure specificity and set a patient up for success, goals must be personal, realistic, and meaningful to the patient. An excellent and reliable way to do this is by helping the patient create a SMART goal. These goals are

- **s**pecific,
- **m**easurable,
- **a**ttainable,
- **r**ealistic, and
- **t**imely.

The following are examples of common patient goals that can be transformed into SMART goals.

Example SMART Goals for Weight Loss

Weight loss is a common self-determined patient goal. Although their goal is important, establishing it without any parameters is insufficient. The provider also must guide the patient in developing it into a well-defined, impactful SMART goal by helping them determine how they plan to lose weight. The patient would develop a SMART goal to state, "I want to lose five pounds in the next month by decreasing my daily calories from 2,500 to 2,000," which gives them a structured plan. Now, knowing how the patient wants to achieve the goal, the provider can help them with a referral to a nutritionist.

Another example of transforming a generic goal of weight loss into a SMART goal is, "I want to lose five pounds in the next month by purchasing healthier foods." This statement may prompt the provider to ask the patient about their financial capability to purchase healthy food, which may lead to a referral to a social worker to assist the patient with food resources. The patient feels supported by the team and views its members as invested in their goal. The team is focused on the patient's goal rather than the provider's wishes and objectives for the patient. SMART goals developed by the patient, focused on their personal preferences, lead to higher patient commitment and compliance, thereby increasing their success rate. SMART goals put the patient in the driver's seat, with the primary care team in the passenger seat holding the map to the destination.

SMART Goals Depending on Diagnosis

Patients may struggle to come up with SMART goals on their own. The primary care team can facilitate this by using a worksheet suited to patients' diagnoses. The patient first should be asked what diagnosis concerns them the most. If they are uncertain, the provider can guide the patient through education on each diagnosis. This is the provider's opportunity to discuss the implications of poor outcomes and use these to guide the patient in prioritizing concerns. Once the patient has been educated about the disease process or illness, the provider can then aid them in creating a significant goal that will have the greatest impact on the patient's specific situation.

Exhibit 3.2 offers examples of SMART goals for commonly seen diagnoses. It gives patients concrete examples of activities for reaching their SMART goals. Along with these examples, the worksheet should have sections for the patient to answer the following questions:

- How will you complete your goal?
- In what amount of time will you complete your goal?
- How important is your goal to you?
- What are the barriers to reaching your goal?
- How can you overcome these barriers?
- How can your primary care team help?

This last question is crucial to aiding in patient success, as it gives them the chance to convey any perceived barriers. The primary care team can use this information

Exhibit 3.2: SMART Goal Examples

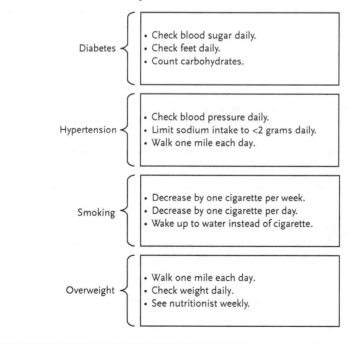

Diabetes	• Check blood sugar daily. • Check feet daily. • Count carbohydrates.
Hypertension	• Check blood pressure daily. • Limit sodium intake to <2 grams daily. • Walk one mile each day.
Smoking	• Decrease by one cigarette per week. • Decrease by one cigarette per day. • Wake up to water instead of cigarette.
Overweight	• Walk one mile each day. • Check weight daily. • See nutritionist weekly.

to give the patient options or interventions to help overcome these barriers and remain on the road to success.

Ideally the patient should be given the SMART goals worksheet prior to the visit. The intent is to have the patient thoughtfully complete the worksheet before seeing the provider so they both can spend time discussing the goal. Follow-up telephone visits with the RN are useful for checking in with the patient and monitoring their progress. The goal for the primary care team is to assist each patient in establishing a SMART goal through guidance and education no later than one week after the patient's visit. Please see appendix A for an easy-to-use SMART goal worksheet for a patient with diabetes, modeled after the Joint Commission Self-Management Goals Worksheet.

Comprehensive Care Through Assessment and Care Plans

To create a comprehensive care plan, the primary care team must focus on treating the patient as a whole.

Mental, Emotional, Social, and Financial Assessment

To provide comprehensive care within the PCMH, the patient's mental, emotional, social, and financial needs must be addressed through screening tools. Understanding how these factors can affect the patient's individual situation is critical, as they all can become barriers to goal achievement.

> **Pearl 3: Assess the impact of mental, emotional, social, and financial needs on the patient's healthcare goal.**

Exhibit 3.3 offers screening tools and questions that are effective in assessing additional needs.

Exhibit 3.3: Screening for Additional Needs

Need	Screening Tools
Mental	Patient Health Questionnaire–9 (depression screen)
	Alcohol Use Disorders Identification Test–Concise (alcohol screening)
Emotional	Perceived Stress Scale
Social	Are you worried about having enough food?
	Are you worried about losing your home? Do you have a home?
Financial	Do you need help with finding employment?

Creating the Care Plan

Once the patient has created a SMART goal and the primary care team has assessed them for additional needed resources, a comprehensive care plan can be created and customized with the patient. Keep in mind there is no single template that must be used or followed when developing a care plan.

Let us check in on Mr. Roberts: After his initial visit with his provider, Mr. Roberts decides to see the nutritionist and start two different oral medications. His screening for stressors reveals he lacks the social support needed to help him cope with diabetes and likely would benefit from a shared medical appointment, where he can be treated in a group environment with patients who have the same diagnosis.

Exhibit 3.4 is an example of a comprehensive care plan for Mr. Roberts that incorporates his need for dietary education.

Shortly after initiating medication, he develops side effects and plans to stop taking it. This happened when he trialed the same medication years ago. He begins to feel defeated again, as he had been experiencing decreased blood sugar levels and had thought the medication, combined with his new diet, was working. He leaves a voicemail for the RN on his primary care team to let her know that he plans to stop the medication.

Pearl 4: Reassess and adjust the care plan.

The RN connects with Mr. Roberts to ask additional questions. She learns that he was in fact having success with the medication, but the side effects were starting to outweigh the benefits. The RN communicates this to the provider, who recommends involving the pharmacist to assist with medication tolerability.

Exhibit 3.5 depicts how the RN updates the care plan to reflect the changes.

Exhibit 3.4: Mr. Roberts's Comprehensive Care Plan

Patient: Mr. Roberts
SMART Goal: Control diabetes (HbA1c <7%) with oral medication over the next 12 months

Medication	Barriers	Resources	Follow-Ups
Metformin Januvia	Needs carbohydrate education Lacks social support	Nutritionist Shared medical appointment	Weekly Monthly

---

Exhibit 3.5: Updated Plan

Patient: Mr. Roberts			
SMART Goal: Control diabetes (HbA1c <7%) with oral medication over the next 12 months			
Medication	**Barriers**	**Resources**	**Follow-Ups**
Metformin	Needs carbohydrate	Nutritionist	Weekly
Januvia	education	Shared medical	
	Lacks social support	appointment	Monthly
	Poor tolerance to	Pharmacist	Weekly
	medication		

This scenario illustrates the need to review the care plan with the patient during each follow-up visit and frequently between visits. Follow-up visits and check-ins provide opportunities for the primary care team to assess for new obstacles and determine patient-centered solutions. The care plan can then be updated to ensure the patient remains on course for success.

Facilitating Coordinated Care

Case Study Continued: After the RN updates the care plan for Mr. Roberts to reflect his issues with medication side effects, she coordinates involvement by the pharmacist. The pharmacist learns that the medication is effective for Mr. Roberts but he is not willing to continue it because of its side effects. The pharmacist recommends changing the medication to an extended-release form, indicated for patients who experience these specific side effects, which will allow Mr. Roberts to remain on a medication that is successfully lowering his blood sugar. The pharmacist schedules a weekly check-in with the patient to ensure his side effects subside. Noting that the patient's care plan also has a nutrition appointment scheduled, the pharmacist reaches out to the nutritionist to inform her of the side effects so that Mr. Roberts's dietary plan can be tailored as well. Without the care plan and effective communication, the patient may have stopped an effective medication because they did not know there is an alternative solution. By discussing the patient's side effects with the nutritionist, a modified plan is created, allowing the patient to stay on track for reaching his goals.

Avoiding Poorly Coordinated Care

A lack of coordinated care can be detrimental to patient outcomes, especially when hospitalized. When there is a breakdown in communication between the primary care team and the hospital team, damaging consequences can occur, especially for a patient with a chronic disease. Communication breakdowns are one of the most common causes of medical errors and high readmission rates.

Case Study Continued: Mr. Roberts is hospitalized for a severe foot injury after a motor vehicle accident. While in the hospital, he informs the emergency room physician that he is taking a diabetes medication but does not remember the name. Unable to determine which medication, the physician starts him on a medication different from what Mr. Roberts is currently taking. Learning that Mr. Roberts has been hospitalized, the RN contacts the hospital to communicate with the physician by using a specific instrument called the situation, background, assessment, and recommendation (SBAR) tool.

Although commonly used in the hospital setting, the SBAR tool is a template that also can be implemented by the primary care team RN to provide a concise report of the patient's current health status. The SBAR tool ensures that the needed information is communicated to the individuals who are now involved in the patient's care. Ideally this type of communication occurs whenever there is a change in level of care between hospitals, skilled nursing facilities, and the primary care setting.

> The SBAR tool ensures that the needed information is communicated to the individuals who are now involved in the patient's care.

Exhibit 3.6 shows the information communicated by the RN to the hospital on Mr. Roberts's behalf during his hospitalization.

Now that the emergency room physician knows the type of medication Mr. Roberts is taking, the inpatient medication plan is adjusted to keep him on his current regimen. The physician also writes orders to start checking Mr. Roberts's blood glucose throughout his stay. Additionally, while Mr. Roberts is in the hospital, a nutritionist is consulted to ensure he is placed on a diet tailored to the needs of his diabetes. Last, thanks to the disclosure of a

Exhibit 3.6: Information Communicated by Registered Nurse to Hospital

SBAR for Mr. Roberts	
Situation	Diabetes, currently taking metformin and Januvia
Background	Diabetes for 20 years with prior foot ulcers
Assessment	Currently uncontrolled with HbA1c of 9%
Recommendation	Benefit from nutrition consult and podiatry consult while inpatient

prior foot ulcer, a referral to a podiatrist is ordered at discharge. Because the SBAR enabled good communication, Mr. Roberts's inpatient care is well coordinated, allowing him to remain on track with his diabetes goals. Following discharge, his coordinated care continues as he is referred to an outpatient podiatrist to help prevent the development of any wounds or complications. Far too often, inadequate communication and poorly coordinated care cause adverse patient events and worsening of patient conditions.

Pre-appointment Planning

Pre-appointment planning can help make coordination of care and the patient visit go smoothly. When information is collected before the patient visit, the patient and provider have more time to focus on patient needs.

Case Study Continued: After being discharged, Mr. Roberts is scheduled for a follow-up visit with his primary care team. In preparation for this visit, he receives a call from the LPN one week before the appointment.

Pearl 5: Prepare for a successful visit.

The LPN asks about the concerns or questions he plans to discuss during his appointment. Mr. Roberts reports he is having trouble walking long distances and would like a Department of Motor Vehicles (DMV) disability placard. Knowing this request in advance, the LPN obtains the DMV forms ahead of time and gives them to the provider to review for Mr. Roberts. She has also requested the records from his recent hospitalization and notes that a referral to an outpatient podiatrist was recommended. The LPN documents this for the provider to ensure that the referral is ordered during the upcoming follow-up visit. Proper preparation ahead of the visit allows the provider to save time and gives a patient the impression that their care team is well prepared for the visit. Mr. Roberts walks out of his appointment with a referral for podiatry and a completed application for a DMV disability placard.

Had the LPN not completed pre-appointment preparation, the provider and team would have wasted valuable time obtaining the DMV form and hospital records. This loss of time can result in delays in care and an unfavorable perception of the quality of care provided.

Prepping

Usually completed by the LPN/LVN one week before the appointment, prepping patient charts is an effective way to prepare for each patient visit. The purpose

Exhibit 3.7: Appointment Prep Checklist

Appointment Prep Checklist for Patient:	Y	N
1. Are the needed labs/imaging complete?		
2. Obtained needed forms?		
3. Obtained hospital discharge records (if applicable)?		

of prepping is to ensure there are no gaps that could affect the patient visit. The process identifies the reason for a patient appointment and determines what the patient and provider need for a successful visit.

Exhibit 3.7 lists example questions to help the LPN/LVN prep each patient appointment. For a comprehensive prepping checklist, see appendix B.

In some settings, the scheduler can assist with obtaining some of the information required to prep successfully for an appointment by helping with insurance information and forms/documents/records retrieval. The scheduler can also coordinate the right type of appointment for the patient, taking patient preference into account.

Improving Access with Telemedicine and Shared Medical Appointments

Ensuring access means the patient has several opportunities to interact with the primary care team on a timely and convenient basis. In a constantly changing healthcare environment, the way in which healthcare organizations communicate to patients and monitor them must evolve. Organizations have been able to adapt through offering shared medical appointments, telemedicine, and telehealth services.

Telemedicine provides efficient and comprehensive clinical care that is delivered from a distance. Telehealth differs in that it refers to additional supportive services. These two remote services are best used when a physical exam is not needed and when a patient only requires a quick visit or check-in with their provider or primary care team.

- Tele*medicine* provides clinical services.
- Tele*health* provides additional supportive services.

When to Use Telemedicine or Telehealth

When establishing these services, it should be clear when it is appropriate to use telemedicine or telehealth versus a face-to-face appointment. Exhibit 3.8 provides an example of scenarios, given chronic diagnoses, where these can be applied.

Exhibit 3.8: Telemedicine vs. Telehealth

Telemedicine
Offered by: Primary care provider, RN, or LPN/LVN when collecting data
Diabetes: Blood sugar log review with medication change Headaches: Medication and headache diary review Hypertension: Blood pressure log review with medication changes Communicating Results: Labs or imaging
Telehealth
Offered by: Psychiatry, Nutritionist, Dermatology, Pharmacy, etc.
Depression: Mental health check-in Heart Failure: Initiating low-sodium diet Dermatitis: Visual inspection of chronic rash Chronic Kidney Disease: Review of safe over-the-counter medication with a pharmacist

The Convenience of Shared Medical Appointments

Case Study Continued: After a follow-up visit with his provider, Mr. Roberts returns to the front desk to relay to the scheduler that he needs an appointment with a podiatrist and nutritionist. He also requests to see a diabetes educator. When the scheduler offers him an appointment for each service, Mr. Roberts expresses concern that he will not be able to get the needed time off from work to make all three of these individual appointments. To accommodate him, the scheduler offers a shared medical appointment (SMA) for patients with diabetes. Mr. Roberts is informed that during the SMA, a podiatrist, nutritionist, and diabetes educator will be present to address his concerns. He also learns that other patients with diabetes will be in attendance. This appeals to Mr. Roberts as none of his family or friends have diabetes, making it difficult for them to understand and support him with his healthcare journey. He agrees to be scheduled for the SMA.

Shared Medical Appointment Implementation

SMAs come in three main types. A hybridized version also can be conducted depending on the patient's needs, the type of patients being seen, and the primary care team's comfort level. It may be easier to start with one of the following main types and then adjust over time.

Diagnosis-based shared medical appointment. This type of SMA is offered monthly and is designed for larger groups of more than 15 patients. Such SMAs are typically tailored to patients with the same diagnosis, such as diabetes, high blood pressure, or heart failure. The focus of a diagnosis-based SMA is an educational piece with a question-and-answer session, followed by individualized time with the provider. Various topics can be addressed, including disease-specific nutrition, medication concerns (e.g., regimens, dosing, complications, and properly taking the medication), disease complications, and any educational components specific to the disease process for the group.

Exhibit 3.9 is an example of a diagnosis-based SMA for heart failure.

In this model, the facilitator can be any member of the primary care team. Requirements for Medicare coding are also satisfied, as each patient receives individual time with the provider. See appendix C for a detailed SMA appointment guide for the patient with diabetes.

Drop-in shared medical appointment. Another type of SMA is the drop-in group medical appointment, in which patients move from one team member to the next depending on their needs. The provider can see the patients one on one as they arrive or before they leave. This works best with a medium-size group of 10 to 15 patients and is typically led by multiple members of the primary care team. This SMA pulls all of the team members into the visit, making them all available to the patient during this designated time. The drop-in SMA may be more convenient for patients with time constraints.

Exhibit 3.10 provides a template for how to coordinate this SMA as a one-stop shop given the available services in the clinic. The example is for a hypertensive patient who arrives at 8:00 and moves across each station with the different primary care team members.

Exhibit 3.10 illustrates how effective this type of SMA can be. The patient has basically combined five separate visits with the nurse, nutritionist, social worker, provider, and pharmacist into one coordinated, comprehensive, and complete visit.

Exhibit 3.9: Diagnosis-Based Shared Medical Appointment Schedule

8:00	Patient arrival	
8:15	Facilitator welcomes patients	
8:30	Educational presentations	
	8:30–9:00	Medication review (pharmacist)
	9:00–9:30	Sodium restrictions (nutritionist)
	9:30–10:00	Signs of fluid retention and what to do (RN)
10:00	Q&A	
10:30	Provider gives individualized care to patients in adjacent exam room	
11:30	Determine topic for next heart failure session depending on the needs of the group	
12:00	Adjourn	

Exhibit 3.10: Drop-In Shared Medical Appointment

8:00	Patient arrives
8:15	LPN/LVN obtains vitals and determines what the patient needs
8:30	RN reviews recently obtained vital signs and blood pressure log. Education is provided on how to properly check blood pressure
8:45	Nutritionist discusses low-sodium diet to help lower blood pressure
9:15	Social worker provides resources for low-sodium food
9:30	Provider gives individualized care to the patient and makes medication adjustment
9:45	Pharmacist reviews medication change, assesses for possible interactions, educates the patient on how to properly time meds, and assesses for any barriers to taking medication
10:00	Scheduler makes follow-up telemedicine visit with RN for repeat blood pressure check

Shared medical appointments for acute concerns. SMAs for acute concerns are best suited for a smaller group of patients who are scheduled every 15 to 30 minutes and have specific concerns. All patients spend individual time with the provider for physical exams, followed by group time to discuss their concerns. Because this type of group visit is not specific to a disease process, and therefore patient questions can vary more widely, a smaller group size of five patients or less is recommended. Any patient with any type of medical issue can participate in this type of SMA, which provides the perfect environment for patients to check in and discuss any new or acute issues.

Exhibit 3.11 provides examples of SMAs for groups of patients with particular acute concerns. Patients are first seen by the provider in 15-minute increments in individual exam rooms; they are then brought together for the group-visit portion to focus on their questions.

Exhibit 3.11: Acute-Concerns Shared Medical Appointment

8:00–9:00	Patient A knee pain Patient B back pain Patient C neck pain Patient D wrist pain
9:00–10:00	Q&A with provider for additional pain management options such as meditation, stretching, alternating hot and cold therapy, topical pain alleviators, etc.

This format can be altered to have the Q&A session run concurrently with the physical exams, but it would need to be conducted by another team member such as the RN. However, such a format would be more efficient, as patients would not need to wait for the provider to finish with all of the attendees; instead, the patients can filter in and out of the Q&A session as needed.

Tailoring the SMA to the Provider and Patient Population

After years of conducting SMAs, observing other SMAs, and coaching colleagues to establish SMAs in their clinics, I (Gina) have seen a wide variation in SMA formats designed for the provider's comfort level and the specific patient population. Over time, and with the addition of new services, my own SMAs have evolved to be a combination of the drop-in and diagnosis-based SMA.

Exhibit 3.12, a tailored approach to SMAs for patients with diabetes complications, is the template of what I have found to be successful for my patients. It provides a step-by-step approach of what happens from the moment the patient

---

Exhibit 3.12: SMA: Tailored for Patients with Diabetes

8:00–8:15	Patient check-in, vital signs taken by LPN/LVN, patients placed in the group care room and start socializing. This must be done by multiple LPNs/LVNs or medical assistants to room all patients within 15 minutes.
8:15–11:15	Review each individual patient's glucose log on a white board with medication changes. This is a critical education piece where patients learn from each other's blood sugar logs and start to understand what their numbers mean and how to make corrections. It is set up in a classroom setting, which lends itself to robust Q&A and discussions. The time varies depending on the number of patients in attendance. Caregivers are also welcome in this setting.
11:15–12:00	Nutritionist tailors dietary education depending on the needs of the patients and is also able to give tailored advice.
12:00–12:30	Video conference is used to bring in a pharmacist from another clinic. She discusses how medication works and troubleshoots any medication concerns.
12:30–12:45	During the SMA, the LVN/LPN has checked each patient chart to ensure retinal eye exam, labs, and foot exam are up to date. If not, the patient is able to see the podiatrist and tele-retinal health technician if needed before leaving. If updated labs are needed, patients are able to get this done prior to leaving as well. The LVN/LPN gives patients a check-out sheet with any needed additional services, which the scheduler can coordinate before the patient leaves.

Note: Patient consent is obtained prior to each SMA because private health information is discussed.

checks-in for the appointment to the end of the visit. This specific model allows for up to 15 patients to be seen. This SMA template is specifically designed for patients with complex diabetes who have had difficulty controlling their diabetes and need more frequent check-ins.

SMAs provide the highest level of organized care for our patients, creating an experience that is well organized, comprehensive, and efficient. For a form that further enhances this experience for the providers, see appendix D, the SMA preparation checklist. When the LVN or LPN completes this form during the prepping process, the provider is able to conduct the appointment seamlessly.

Benefits of Shared Medical Appointments

The following are highlights of the benefits I personally have seen for patients who attend SMAs:

- More time spent focused on barriers to controlling diabetes.
- Patients provide peer support and accountability to each other.
- HbA1c goals are realized more quickly.
- Coordinated care with pharmacy, podiatry, nutritionist, and tele-retinal technician provides tailored patient care.
- Patients learn from each other.
- Increased access to care.
- Patient buy-in is greater.

The benefits to the organization are as follows:

- Fewer diabetes complications in complex patients because of frequent interventions.
- Increased cooperation as supporting team members are incorporated across each clinic, such as using the pharmacist in one clinic to provide remote education in another.
- Patient satisfaction is increased.
- Increased enrollment as other services recommend patients attend our SMA.
- Quality metrics are improved.
- Greater utilization of services.

SMAs are the ultimate form of patient-centered healthcare delivery.

Impact of COVID-19 on PCMHs

Because of COVID-19, telemedicine is no longer a novelty but rather a necessity. With social distancing and quarantining requirements and recommendations, organizations have adapted by transitioning to deliver nontraditional, virtual appointments. Except for patients whose specific circumstances require an in-person physical exam, all patient visits are conducted via video or telephone. Through telemedicine, the primary care team can still connect with and monitor patients effectively, and the patients feel safer seeing their team from the safety of their own homes.

Telemedicine is not without its challenges, though, as patients still need to have lab work completed and vital signs taken, but the process is continuing to evolve and improve. Although there is no virtual alternative for most lab work, we are seeing changes in the collection of vital signs, as patients can measure their own weight, temperature, and blood pressure and provide them to the LPN or LVN during the pre-appointment call. Supportive services such as nutritionists, pharmacists, social workers, and mental/behavioral healthcare specialists also have been able to transition successfully to virtual care.

The social distancing requirements resulting from COVID-19 also have hampered the ability to provide SMAs, but these appointments can be conducted virtually as well. In my own experience, SMAs for patients with diabetes or hypertension have continued with patients providing their own data, as discussed in the preceding examples. For example, in the hypertension SMA, patients will check their own blood pressure and provide their readings while the facilitator watches them take it.

To successfully navigate the environment created by COVID-19, each healthcare organization must be flexible and evolve their process to ensure access while providing high-quality patient care.

Continuously Assessing and Improving Quality and Safety

Quality care and patient safety must be constantly measured, assessed, and improved. The Donabedian model provides a framework for examining quality in healthcare as a continuous process. According to this model, quality is defined and assessed using a three-part structure. This will be further explained in chapter 8, "Key Performance Indicators." Exhibit 3.13 breaks down the Donabedian model.

> Measuring quality is critical for determining how well a process is working. It identifies what does and does not work while creating opportunities for improvements and sharing best practices.

Measuring quality is critical for determining how well a process is working. It identifies what does and does not work while creating opportunities for improvements and sharing best practices. To

Exhibit 3.13: Donabedian Model for Evaluating Quality in Healthcare

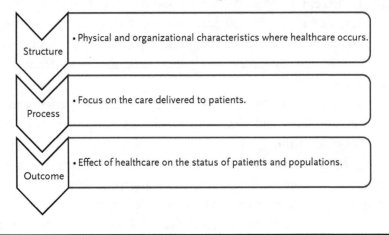

Structure • Physical and organizational characteristics where healthcare occurs.

Process • Focus on the care delivered to patients.

Outcome • Effect of healthcare on the status of patients and populations.

effectively measure quality, the organization must have a database for data collection and definitions, and a process for extrapolating data that ensures proper measurement. It is also important to have staff engagement and understanding of why measuring quality and safety is important. See chapter 8 for more information on selecting strong information systems, details on key performance indicators, and how to gain staff involvement.

KEY POINTS

- A successful PCMH incorporates the five core elements.
- Patient-centered care can be enhanced through SMART goals.
- Comprehensive care can be tailored through care plans.
- Pre-appointment planning is vital to facilitating coordinated care.
- SMAs ensure access by incorporating several team members in one visit.
- Quality and safety must be continuously monitored and improved to ensure value-based care and good outcomes.

RESOURCES

Agency for Healthcare Research and Quality. 2015. "Types of Health Care Quality Measures." www.ahrq.gov/talkingquality/measures/types.html.

American Academy of Family Physicians. 2021. "Shared Medical Appointments/Group Visits." www.aafp.org/about/policies/all/shared-medical-appointments.html.

American Academy of Physician Assistants. 2021. "Shared Medical Appointments." www.aapa.org/career-central/employer-resources/shared-medical-appointments.

Berwick, D., and D. Fox. 2016. "Evaluating the Quality of Medical Care: Donabedian's Classic Article 50 Years Later." *Milbank Quarterly: A Journal of Population Health and Health Policy* 94 (2): 237–41.

Centers for Disease Control and Prevention. 2021. "STEPS to Care: Care Plans." www.cdc.gov/hiv/effective-interventions/treat/steps-to-care/dashboard/care-plans.html.

Jordan, L. 2017. "Health Literacy, Self-Management Goals Made Simple." Presentation at The Joint Commission Conference, April 6.

Moore, L., A. Lavoie, B. Gilles, and J. Lapointe. 2015. "Donabedian's Structure-Process-Outcome Quality of Care Model: Validation in an Integrated Trauma System." *Journal of Trauma and Acute Care Surgery* 78 (6): 1168–75.

National Committee for Quality Assurance. 2021. "Patient-Centered Medical Home (PCMH)." www.ncqa.org/programs/health-care-providers-practices/patient-centered-medical-home-pcmh.

US Department of Health and Human Services. 2020. "About Healthcare Quality." https://health.gov/our-work/health-care-quality/about-health-care-quality.

CHAPTER 4

Staff Engagement

LET ME (MARY-ELLEN) share an example of a personal healthcare experience that demonstrates staff engagement. Recently I needed to make an appointment for medical clearance from my primary care provider for a minor surgical procedure. I arrived a few minutes ahead of schedule on a Saturday morning. (Yes, my provider offers appointments on the weekend!)

As I entered the waiting room, I noticed a sign indicating that flu shots were available on a walk-in basis. I made a note to ask the nurse if I could get this taken care of during my visit.

I had barely sat down when a nurse emerged with a smile on her face and called my first name. She gave me a warm greeting, stating, "I am going to make this an awesome visit for you today." *Wow*, I thought, *I've never heard that before.*

She proceeded to take my vitals and explain what would happen during my visit. I asked about the flu shot and she confirmed that I would be able to get it. As she left the exam room, she indicated that the physician assistant (PA) would be in to see me very soon. Sure enough, within minutes, the PA entered the room, likewise greeting me warmly while explaining what she would be doing to complete my visit.

The rest of the visit went like clockwork, and, as I made my way out of the exam area, the nurse and PA, both smiling, waved goodbye. I think you would agree that mine was truly an "awesome" visit. Granted, this was a Saturday schedule, not a busy weekday. But the way they made me feel, in that moment, was special, and all it took was a focus on me and my needs.

LEADERSHIP

Staff engagement starts with good leadership. Staff members value leaders who are ethical, transparent, and inclusive; those who give them meaningful work and provide positive workplace experiences. These leaders foster teamwork, collaboration, and continuous learning while providing coaching and feedback.

In the primary care clinics that we operate, our governance structure is designed to be inclusive. Our Performance Excellence Team acts as the governing body, providing oversight and support to planning, operations, monitoring, evaluation, and continuous process improvement. Staff from all clinics, at all levels of the organization, participate as members or ad hoc presenters.

The next level of the management structure includes key committees:

- Credentialing & Privileging Review Board
- Environment of Care Committee
- Infection Prevention & Control Team
- Women's Health Committee
- Peer Review Team

Staff have the opportunity to serve on these groups, learning and developing new skills as they participate, and making contributions of their own.

THE IMPORTANCE OF ONBOARDING

How do we connect our staff to purpose so that their aim is to make every visit for every patient an awesome experience? It starts with recruitment and onboarding. Do staff seek out a position in your facility because the community holds it in high regard? What is your organization's image and what story about it do your current employees tell their friends and neighbors? Is it a good place to work, supportive of staff with an environment that promotes growth and learning? These are good discussion questions for your leadership group.

Interviewing and onboarding are the first opportunities to share the organization's values and set expectations for behaviors that demonstrate those values. Performance and behavioral-based interviews help to identify potential hires whose experience and values resonate with yours. These values also can be codified in customer service standards.

Be sure to give your candidates ample time to interview you as well. You should anticipate that they will have expectations for the position, the organization, and their experience as an employee.

Last, pairing your new hire with a mentor or peer can smooth the way in the first 120 days.

CREATING AND IMPLEMENTING CUSTOMER EXPERIENCE STANDARDS

One of the first things we did as we stood up the initial group of primary care clinics was to establish standards for how staff would interact with our patients at key service points: phone calls, check-in, and the provider visit. Just as important were standards for how they interacted with each other that would demonstrate respect and professionalism.

Knowing that this effort could not be top down, we chartered a team of high-performing staff members from various disciplines to create these standards. After reviewing examples from well-known primary care organizations, the team developed sets of standards that were shared with staff at all our clinics. The team used feedback from other staff to refine their product. The final version is now displayed at every clinic, presented during orientation, discussed at staff meetings, and coached by clinic managers.

Additional points of integration for these standards include job descriptions, performance appraisals, and recognition efforts. We take it a step further by connecting our patient stories to specific customer experience standards, making them part of what we do every day.

CONNECTING TO PURPOSE

Most people choose healthcare because they want to serve others, to make a difference. Yet too often, in the busy operations of the clinic setting, staff lose sight of that purpose. How do we keep them connected so they can deliver their very best to our patients?

We start during transition week when we are opening a new clinic. In small group discussions, I ask each employee why they chose healthcare for their career and to think about what would happen to the patient if they did not do their job. Their answers and the discussion that follows powerfully remind them of their commitment to serving patients and the significance of their work.

Similarly, we start each staff meeting with a patient story. It might be a success story, a near-miss, or a time when we didn't meet a patient's expectations. Safety is the theme of the stories based on adverse events. Staff members rotate monthly as presenters, sharing their story and starting a discussion, using effective questions:

- What went well? Let's make sure we hardwire the practices that made it a positive experience.
- What could we have done better?
- What are the lessons learned?

The stories keep staff focused on the patient, and the questions establish an environment of continuous learning and process improvement. I suggest inviting a patient to attend your meetings and share a story about their experience in your clinic. Hearing it directly from the patient can be very powerful.

THE "WHY"

We owe it to our staff to give them the rationale behind decisions and include them in the decision-making process as often as possible. Employee surveys tell us that one of the main reasons for dissatisfaction is not being included in decisions that affect their work.

Let me share a story to illustrate the impact of "why." My son gave me a smartphone for Mother's Day and pays my monthly bill. He likes to receive photos and messages when I vacation in Europe and Asia. He had asked that I make these transmissions using my hotel's Wi-Fi.

Excited to share my experiences in real time, I often disregarded his request and sent photos and texts while out sightseeing. Later he explained the rationale behind his request. Because we are both on the same phone plan, when I send and he receives, it's a double hit on the data limit, and charges add up quickly. Using the hotel Wi-Fi cuts this in half. Once I understood the "why," my behavior changed.

How do our messages satisfy the "why"? Presenting the rational side (the evidence), the emotional side (the heart), and the personal side (what's in it for me) helps staff to understand and connect.

Recently we implemented a new weekly reporting process and template for our medical service associates (MSAs). At first, the MSAs in one of our clinics were resistant, seeing it as micromanagement and busy work. When our chief quality manager explained that it was a tool to help them stay organized and keep track of patients, they jumped on board.

High-stress environments and situations, such as the COVID-19 pandemic, can cause staff to lose their connection to purpose, resulting in compassion fatigue and burnout. In fact, Dzau, Kirch, and Nasca (2020) describe the physical and emotional harm experienced by healthcare professionals who are caring for COVID-19 patients as a parallel pandemic.

How do we nurture the well-being of our staff while building emotional resilience? Here is an example from Puran (2020): the six-word story. Staff were invited to submit six-word stories on their inspiration in choosing a career in healthcare. Remembering your "why" is especially important during difficult times. Sharing stories is a powerful way to make connections and build teams.

I tried this exercise with our clinic staff. Here are a few six-word stories they shared:

- Making a difference in people's lives.
- Natural-born caregivers, keeping the tradition.
- Science combined with compassion—perfect job!
- Serving those who served us.
- Helping to maintain health and happiness.
- Following in my big sister's footsteps.

The process of reflection, sharing stories, and supporting each other was powerful. These stories served as a reminder of the individual's "why" while providing a space for camaraderie and empathy.

BURNOUT AND RESILIENCE

How do we effectively manage staff burnout so that we can build resilience? Start by identifying and pausing or removing non–value-added initiatives, meetings, and tasks that decrease staff capacity. Ask staff what these are; they know.

Don't get caught up in "flavor of the month" churn-and-burn behaviors. Be focused and act strategically as your organization takes on new initiatives. Employ multidirectional communication that is targeted and laser focused. Don't inundate your staff with a ton of useless information, but don't leave them out of the loop either.

Develop staff wellness programs with their input so you know you are hitting the mark. Options include on-site healthy food selections, initiatives and competitions that reward healthy behaviors, support groups, and employee assistance programs. (I know of an organization that provides staff with QR codes to make their own healthcare appointments.) Also, post motivational, positive messages in staff areas to lift their spirits during difficult days.

Being intentional about compassion can relieve burnout. Evidence shows (Mazzarelli and Trzeciak 2019) that exercising compassion leads to a better quality of life while increasing people's sense of personal accomplishment.

What is compassion? Mazzarelli and Trzeciak (2019) theorize that it is empathy plus action: we tune into the feelings of others and take specific steps to address those feelings. Compassion releases the mind from the harmful effects of negative emotion and connects us to purpose. Compassion always matters; it is a necessity in healthcare. Just 40 seconds is all it takes to confer

> Compassion always matters; it is a necessity in healthcare.

the benefits that compassion provides, and it is a skill that can be practiced and learned.

How do we show compassion?

- Eye-level contact
- Removing physical barriers
- Open posture; leaning in
- Concerned facial expression
- Active listening; showing support
- Acknowledging the other person's pain
- Self-compassion: extending compassion to yourself in times of suffering and distress

JOY IN THE WORKPLACE

When staff connect to purpose and demonstrate their commitment, it can be a joyful experience. By contrast, getting caught up in day-to-day tasks, frustrations, and the rapid pace of healthcare delivery can distract them from their purpose and rob them of this joy.

Staff meetings make good venues to have conversations that include envisioning, issue identification, and problem solving. The dialogue, as suggested by the Institute for Healthcare Improvement (Perlo et al. 2017), could go like this:

- What makes a good day for you?
- What makes you proud to work here?
- When we are at our best, what does that look like?

Starting with the positive, the goal, or the aspiration raises the staff's sights and expectations. They talk about what is possible.

Next, the conversation moves to the barriers:

- What are the pebbles in your shoes?
- What makes for a bad day?
- What frustrates you the most?
- What are your improvement suggestions?

Through these questions and discussion points, the staff identify processes they can improve to transform bad days into those days when they are at their best. You can also conduct staff focus groups around persistent process issues to generate innovative solutions.

LEVELS OF STAFF ENGAGEMENT

Given a similar working environment and circumstances, staff often react in different ways, which affects their performance. Exhibit 4.1 depicts the different levels of engagement and their characteristic behaviors as described by Baird (2008).

Astute leaders assess and measure staff performance and engagement levels, support the engaged and fully engaged, and coach the somewhat engaged up or out. The leader's responsibility is to meet their employees critical needs and

---

Exhibit 4.1: Levels of Engagement

Level 1: Disengaged

- Only work when they have to
- They would prefer to be doing something else
- Results are NOT meeting standards
- Have a we–they perspective
- Negative about the organization, as well as their interactions with coworkers and patients

Level 2: Somewhat Engaged

- Selective about where they put their energy
- Spend a lot of time doing things that are not helping patients
- Deliver when they have to, or when you are watching
- Do what it takes to get by
- Masters at distracting others

Level 3: Engaged

- Focused on their deliverables, project, and individual responsibilities
- Deliver good, solid performances
- Always do their fair share
- Work well with others and will help out when asked

Level 4: Fully Engaged

- Passionate about their work and their organization
- Will do whatever it takes to deliver results
- Feel like a true owner
- Delivering consistently high-quality results is their trademark
- Find innovative solutions to the toughest problems
- Seen as a role model or leader

Source: Adapted from Baird (2008).

provide the tools for them to do the job they were hired to do. Employees then choose how engaged they will be.

Staff watch how their managers and leaders respond to those who are disengaged. Although they may not be privy to coaching efforts and should not be informed of others' disciplinary actions, they will expect to see poor behaviors improve over time. If not, managers risk losing the engagement of those who have been consistently good performers.

Fair treatment and accountability, partnered with solid coaching, have the potential to improve performance, which evens the workload and avoids burnout and resentment.

Engagement Surveys

How do we measure staff engagement? A common method is the employee satisfaction (engagement) survey. This tool provides an opportunity for staff to have input into processes, decisions, and conditions that affect their work. Surveys are a confidential and safe avenue to identify the strengths of the organization and opportunities for improvement.

Do you get the maximum potential from your survey efforts? Exhibit 4.2 has a few tips for you to consider.

Exhibit 4.2: Survey Tips

Before the Survey
Prepare the staff for the survey. The best place to initiate the conversation is at your staff meeting. Include the following:
• Rationale for the survey.
• Dates the survey will be available for them to complete and how they will access it.
• Let them know that each survey is confidential and that management will not have access to individual surveys, only the aggregate report.

During the Survey
Make sure every staff member is given protected time and a private space to complete the survey.
Encourage everyone to participate.

After the Survey
When you receive the results, share them at the next staff meeting.
Encourage a robust dialogue, focusing first on the strengths.
Find ways to celebrate the positives.

(continued)

Exhibit 4.2: Survey Tips (*continued*)

Discuss the opportunities for improvement.

Set priorities for capitalizing on strengths and addressing opportunities for improvement.

Ask for volunteers to work in small groups to recommend strategies or actions.

Schedule these teams to report their progress and recommendations at upcoming staff meetings.

Ask staff for solutions that are meaningful with realistic implementation timelines.

Before the Next Survey

Provide a summary of actions taken as a result of the last survey. It is important that staff know their voices were heard and something positive happened as a result.

Encourage everyone to participate in the next survey. The response rate should improve from the prior survey if staff felt that taking it was worthwhile.

Survey results are often just a flag that identifies issues in need of exploration and points you toward further inquiry. Using our survey results, we chartered teams to take a deep dive into employee-engagement, reward and recognition, and provider-retention practices.

The Team Process

The teams examining employee engagement followed a Lean approach to define the current state and describe the target state. They used brainstorming, cause-and-effect diagrams, surveys, and PICK (Possible, Implement, Challenge, Kill) charts to identify and prioritize potential solutions. At the outset we seeded the teams with a leader champion to ensure that their efforts would align with strategic objectives.

When their work was done, the teams presented their storyboards to the leadership team. Exhibit 4.3 lists the changes we made as a result of these efforts.

Here are a few more thoughts on meaningful recognition of staff:

- One size doesn't fit all. Just as we need to personalize and customize our care for patients, staff deserve the same consideration when we are developing our rewards system.
- Include staff in the design process. Who better to construct something meaningful and valued?
- Connect recognition to your customer service standards, strategic goals, and objectives to drive them through the entire organization.

Exhibit 4.3: Changes Enacted Following Teams' Engagement Analysis

Employee Engagement

- Suggestion boxes
- Medical service associates attendance at morning huddle
- Employee mailboxes
- Corporate presence at staff meetings
- Additional communication/training on employee compensation and benefits
- Increased corporate touchpoints with staff
- Initiated a Clinic Newsletter

Reward and Recognition

- Shout-Out Boards
- Plaque to teams for high-level performance on key metrics
- Gift cards with handwritten notes for special acts
- Employee of the Quarter
- Special-occasion food celebrations funded by corporate
- Birthday/anniversary emails
- Kudos in the Clinic Newsletter

- Offer options. A menu of choices puts staff in control with the ability to select what would make them feel special.
- Public recognition shows staff what success looks like. The caveat: Some staff do not enjoy public displays. Know you staff and honor their preferences. Again—personalize!
- Refresh your rewards program regularly. Even the most valued approaches, gestures, and tokens get stale over time.

Ideas for rewards and incentives to recognize employees include the following:

- Peer-to-peer tools: WOW cards, superhero stickers
- Post staff pictures with names and roles to make them feel special
- Social events: staff picnics, morning coffee, ice cream socials, holiday parties
- Patient involvement: comment cards and DAISY Awards
- One-hour time-off coupons
- Handwritten thank-you notes
- Quarterly call or virtual meeting to recognize outstanding staff
- Volunteer-provided yoga classes
- Massages.

This type of teamwork continues in process improvement work. In addition to Lean methodology, we use the plan, do, study, act model to focus on key aspects of clinic operations:

- Second-day post-discharge calls
- Opioid management
- Antimicrobial stewardship
- Communication of diagnostic test results
- Patient missed appointments
- Preventive health screenings

Frontline staff are in the best position to understand, analyze, and improve the processes that drive the delivery of care. These tools serve to engage them as they do this important work.

Our process improvement posters tell the story of the teams' efforts: problem statement, baseline data, improvement actions, and results (See appendix E). We share these posters at staff meetings, during accreditation surveys, and across the clinic enterprise. Improvement work at one clinic is often scalable to the rest.

Culture of Safety

Recently we added questions to our engagement survey to gauge the staff's levels of psychological and physical safety. We strive to create an environment of inquiry and improvement that supports staff in speaking up, asking questions, and making change. We put safety and quality first.

The culture of safety survey asked the following questions:

- I am provided adequate resources and training to provide safe patient care
- I have enough time to complete patient care tasks safely.
- Reporting a patient safety problem will not result in negative repercussions for the person reporting it.
- Necessary steps are taken in my clinic to ensure staff safety.

Using staff feedback on these elements, we made the following improvements:

- Appointed safety officers at every clinic
- Initiated "Toolbox Talks" on safety topics
- Installed additional lighting in the staff parking lot at a clinic in a high-crime area
- Provided coaching to improve teamwork

- Ramped up hiring to fill vacancies
- Clarified roles and assignments

We track our engagement scores across all clinics, year to year. Our results continue to improve by including staff in the process of making their clinics a better place to work.

HIGH-RELIABILITY ORGANIZATIONS

The high-reliability organization (HRO) framework is gaining traction as a way to engage both staff and patients. The goal is zero preventable harm—challenging to meet in such a high-risk environment as healthcare. How do we mitigate these risks, every patient, every day?

By creating a learning system and a just culture of psychological safety, we encourage staff to speak up and raise questions. We connect to the mindfulness of the Whole Health model (see chapter 6) with the following principles, described by Bourne, Peterson, and Veazie (2019) and implemented by many healthcare organizations:

- **Preoccupation with failure:** Anticipating how processes might break down, fixing those weak steps, and correcting process failures fully and immediately, no matter how small.
- **Reluctance to simplify:** Looking for the root causes of a process failure rather than treating the symptoms. Healthcare systems are complex, with complex problems needing complex exploration and solutions.
- **Sensitivity to operations:** Our frontline staff know best the potential and real risks to our patient care processes. Leaders need to create an environment of openness and transparency while being visible and accessible, encouraging staff to speak up and "stop the line" when they have a safety concern. Every voice matters.
- **Commitment to resilience:** The ability to anticipate risks and improvise when the unexpected occurs. Preparing in advance for emergencies will position the healthcare organization to be innovative in a dynamic environment. Certainly this competency was put to the test with the COVID-19 pandemic.
- **Deference to expertise:** Expertise is valued at all levels of the organization in order to identify risks, conduct assessments in a crisis situation, and create solutions.

When staff trust that it's safe to speak up about their concerns, they are more likely to report near-misses and close calls as well as adverse events. Then

Exhibit 4.4: Leading for Safety

Source: Reprinted from American College of Healthcare Executives and IHI/NPSF Lucian Leape Institute (2017).

the learning and improvement can begin. Clear communication, inquiry, and improvement are valued in an HRO (see exhibit 4.4).

Staff Meetings and Huddles

Daily huddles (10–15 minute stand-up meetings) and monthly staff meetings are great venues for incorporating HRO practices and increasing engagement. Build team exercises and educational spots into the agenda as well as shout-outs and celebrations.

As mentioned, invite staff to present on a topic they have been working on. Rotate this responsibility, along with the patient safety story, so that everyone gets a chance to participate. Ask for agenda topics. Use visual management (white boards or electronic huddle boards) to display and track information from huddle to huddle.

The following sample agendas can be used for huddles and staff meetings:

• **Huddle sample agenda**
  – Identification of today's safety risks: methods, equipment, supplies, staff
  – Update on improvement ideas
  – New improvement ideas
  – Key metrics
  – Kudos!

- **Staff meeting sample agenda**
  - Team exercise or icebreaker
  - Patient safety story
  - Educational topic
  - Quality/Patient Safety Report
  - Environmental Safety Officer Report
  - Kudos!

Be sure to take good meeting notes and distribute them to all, especially those who were not able to attend. Follow up and close the loop on pending items so that staff know these meetings are important and you take their input seriously.

Another tool that we have used effectively during staff meetings is the Patient Experience Journey Map developed by the Veterans Healthcare Administration (2019). Staff gather around a large visual that depicts the key touchpoints of a typical patient visit:

- Scheduling an appointment
- Arriving at the clinic and checking in
- Waiting to be seen
- Getting labs or X-rays
- Meeting with the provider
- Check-out

"Bright spots" and "pain points," derived from patient survey feedback, are listed under each touchpoint. Staff discuss what they can do to continue to provide these bright spots while mitigating the pain points.

These robust conversations serve to connect staff to purpose and identify strong practices and areas needing improvement.

An effective strategy to sustain interest and engagement in a specific initiative is to identify a theme of the month and create messages, activities, and stories around it. This will provide new energy and learning as you move toward your implementation goals.

Leader Rounding

As CEO of a large healthcare organization, I quickly came to value the practice of rounding. I took a couple of different approaches. Sitting in a busy clinic and offering to make appointment reminder calls to patients showed that I was willing to help out and gave me insight into routine operations and challenges. In this setting, staff felt comfortable speaking up and asking questions. I learned a lot while identifying things we could do better.

Another effective approach was rounding with clinic managers. My script would go something like this:

- Tell me what you are most proud of in this clinic.
- What could go better?
- Do you have all of the equipment and supplies you need to get the work done?
- Is there anyone in the clinic who has been very supportive lately whom I should recognize?

In an HRO environment, this script expands to include questions about safety and risks. Staff need to know that clinic leadership understands what they face every day and supports them in making necessary improvements. Closing the loop by following up on staff concerns and ideas is critical to effective rounding.

Leader rounding usually does not happen on its own. Too often leaders get caught up in day-to-day tasks, issues, and decisions, so it's important to be intentional about the rounding process. The following is one guide for establishing a rounding process:

- Determine which leader(s) will conduct rounds.
- Decide how frequently they will round.
- Prepare your script.
- Put it on your calendar.

During rounds, leaders ask questions, listen, and identify barriers to the work. They share follow-up on previously identified issues. After rounds, they prioritize the concerns needing a response or action and communicate the plan in timely fashion. Recognizing staff for specific accomplishments or for speaking up about a risk will reinforce a culture of safety. (See appendix F for a sample Leader Rounding form.)

Safety Forums

Regularly scheduled safety forums are another foundational practice of an HRO. They serve to improve the culture and focus attention on what's important. Key attributes of a safety forum include transparency, openness, the courage to speak up, and process examination.

These meetings are focused on problematic/adverse events and the people who manage them—the second victims, who need support when these things happen. Staff need to know that when things go wrong, they will be treated fairly.

Safety forums offer an opportunity to build resilience: how effectively we thrive in our environment. The greatest learning can come through adversity. When things go wrong, do we bounce back rapidly? Why aren't we able to bounce back sometimes? The delay could be linked to systems issues in need of improvement.

The following items comprise a sample safety forum agenda:

- Patient safety story
- HRO education
- Adverse events: lessons learned, outcomes
- Staff recognition (could be for reporting an adverse event, participating in a Root Cause Analysis, stopping the line)

STAFF GROWTH AND DEVELOPMENT

In their engagement surveys, staff told us that they would like to see more opportunities for career advancement within the clinic operations. In response, we are piloting a personal development plan (see appendix G) to align the efforts of staff members with their supervisors'. We also have created opportunities for learning new skill sets. Here are a few examples:

- Safety officer responsibilities are offered as a collateral assignment, with protected time from their primary job to complete the duties. Lab and Radiology techs, nurses, and MSAs step up to take on this role. They participate on our Environment of Care Committee and gain in-depth knowledge as they conduct clinic inspections.
- A licensed practical nurse at one of our clinics demonstrated an interest and ability in data management. Our chief quality manager took this nurse under her wing, partnering with her on designing reports for our key metrics.
- The manager of another clinic invites staff who deliver direct patient care to help out with "back office" functions. She routinely asks staff to present new policies, reports, and patient stories at the monthly staff meeting.
- Our chief quality manager leads teams for Infection Prevention and Control, Women's Health, and Antimicrobial Stewardship. She nurtures the team members by giving them opportunities to take the lead on a given topic.

- The clinical ambassador in each clinic is the liaison between staff and the patient. They identify ways to advocate for the patient while working with staff to improve internal patient-experience processes. They also participate in patient outreach and enrollment events. Again, this is a collateral growth opportunity.
- To support our growing clinics and recognize stellar performance, we created lead nurse care manager and lead MSA positions.

This approach is a win-win for the organization. Staff acquire additional expertise, build new skill sets, and get exposure to various aspects of the clinic operations. It is a pleasure to see them shine as they increase their value to the enterprise.

Our Clinic Newsletter provides a vehicle for showcasing the role of our safety officers and individual and team accomplishments, and tells the stories of staff who have advanced in their careers. The newsletter helps us get the word out that there are multiple paths to advancement in our clinics.

SUPPORTING THE MANAGERS

Let's not forget our managers. Often they have the most difficult job. They must translate goals and objectives to everyday operations, sometimes while acting as the buffer between leadership and the front line.

We have designed a comprehensive approach to grow, nurture, and support our clinic managers. Their regional manager begins working with them during the orientation process to ensure a smooth transition. They are part of a network of clinic managers who share strong practices and challenges as they collaborate to implement change and process improvements.

To ensure they have needed resources at their fingertips, we have created a Clinic Manager's Toolkit. Here is a partial list of resources:

- Customer service standards, coaching tips, and skill-building practice scenarios
- Sample staff meeting agenda, minutes templates, and tips for taking good minutes
- Staff engagement survey tips and action plan template
- The Joint Commission tracer templates/schedule
- Monthly report matrix

The manager group meets weekly with the regional managers, the chief quality officer, and the director to share progress on their metrics, identify opportunities for improvement, and celebrate their successes. They also participate in an annual leadership retreat, which includes educational activities, skill-building labs—and more celebrations!

EMPLOYEE EXPERIENCE

We have talked a lot about employee engagement. Let's take it a step further to the employee experience, which is influenced by every interaction employees have with their coworkers, their supervisor, leadership, and the customers—patients and family members. It starts at recruitment and continues through the life cycle of employment.

We need to put as much effort and emphasis on the employee experience as we do the patient experience. Strong and supportive leadership, learning initiatives, career development opportunities, and staff involvement in designing and improving work processes are key to creating a positive employee experience.

See chapter 6 for self-care and wellness activities that may be applied to staff as well as patients and caregivers, and chapter 7 for a discussion of how designing the clinic environment can enhance the employee experience.

ANOTHER HEALTHCARE STORY

I would like to close this chapter with another personal healthcare experience. After an emergent visit to the ophthalmology office that was covering my provider's practice over the weekend, I called my provider's office to schedule an appointment, as instructed.

After two rings, Lori answered, identifying the practice and herself, and asked how she could help me. Her greeting was warm and friendly. I told her about my weekend visit and that I needed an appointment in four weeks as a follow-up. Right away she had pulled up my record, mentioned that I routinely see Dr. Jones, and that she sees patients on Monday, Tuesday, and Thursday.

She then asked which of those days would be "ideal" for me. I responded, "Thursday," and then she gave me another choice: morning or afternoon. To complete the call, she summarized the appointment information and thanked me for choosing the practice.

In these few minutes, I felt like Lori was focused on my needs and my preferences. Her actions gave me choices. I felt valued as a patient. All it took was a little bit of time and a lot of interest in making this simple interaction "awesome." When employees are engaged, they deliver a better patient experience.

When I told this story to my son, a sometimes-skeptical social worker, he replied, "She was probably scripted to use the word 'ideal.'" That may be, but Lori's manner was genuine and warm. She made me feel cared for. But I agree that we need to be careful about developing scripts for common, routine touchpoints.

The staff need to be the ones developing those scripts, not management. They need to own the process and the words, and practice so they are not robotic. They need to be mindful that every interaction they have with a patient is an opportunity to build trust.

Last, you can help your staff by empowering your patients. Look to chapter 6 for a discussion of patient engagement.

KEY POINTS

- Engagement starts at recruitment and carries through every aspect of a staff member's tenure.
- Customer service standards, designed for expected behaviors, set the bar for performance.
- Intentionally connecting staff to purpose and the "why" promotes engagement.
- Empathy plus action yields compassion.
- A high-reliability organization presents multiple opportunities for staff engagement.
- Creating a culture of safety is a key leadership responsibility.
- Offering a multitude of diverse opportunities helps staff to participate, grow, and develop.
- When employees are engaged, they deliver a better patient experience.

REFERENCES

American College of Healthcare Executives and IHI/NPSF Lucian Leape Institute. 2017. *Leading a Culture of Safety: A Blueprint for Success.* www.ihi.org/resources/ Pages/Publications/Leading-a-Culture-of-Safety-A-Blueprint-for-Success.aspx.

Baird, K. 2008. *Raising the Bar on Service Excellence.* Fort Atkinson, WI: Golden Lamp Press.

Bourne, D., K. Peterson, and S. Veazie. 2019. *Evidence Brief: Implementation of High Reliability Organization Principles.* Published May. Veterans Health Administration, US Department of Veterans Affairs. www.hsrd.research.va.gov/publications/esp/ high-reliability-org.pdf.

Dzau, V., D. Kirch, and T. Nasca. 2020. "Preventing a Parallel Pandemic—a National Strategy to Protect Clinicians' Well-Being." *New England Journal of Medicine* 383 (6): 513–15.

Mazzarelli, A., and S. Trzeciak. 2019. *Compassionomics.* Pensacola, FL: Studer Group.

Perlo, J., B. Balik, S. Swensen, A. Kabcenell, J. Landsman, and D. Feeley. 2017. *IHI Framework for Improving Joy in Work* (IHI white paper). Institute for Healthcare Improvement. www.ihi.org/resources/Pages/IHIWhitePapers/Framework-Improving-Joy-in-Work.aspx.

Puran, A. 2020. "My Six-Word Story: Power to Reconnect and Connect." *Patient Experience Journal* 7 (2): 144–50.

Veterans Healthcare Administration. 2019. "VA Patient Experience Journey Map." US Department of Veterans Affairs. www.blogs.va.gov/VAntage/wp-content/uploads/2019/03/VA-Patient-Experience-Journey-Map.pdf.

CHAPTER 5

Provider Engagement, from a Provider's Point of View

Provider engagement can be challenging for any organization. When providers are not engaged, the organization, team, and patients all suffer. A lack of engagement leads to poor performance with low patient and provider satisfaction scores which causes provider turn over and loss of patients.

This chapter will discuss six strategies for facilitating provider engagement and provide tools to guide relationship building and involvement. These six strategies are not what you would typically find when researching provider engagement. Ironically, many of the tools and tips that have been developed are not from providers themselves.

As a provider who worked in direct patient care for over ten years and then transitioned to quality management, these are the strategies that I (Gina) have learned over time which were successful for myself and my peers.

The six strategies to successful provider engagement are:

- Determine what is meaningful to providers.
- Offer a platform for collegial communication.
- Make leadership accessible.
- Tap into friendly competition.
- Provide opportunities for growth.
- Protect against burnout.

KEY POINT: MONEY DOES NOT EQUAL JOB SATISFACTION

If you were to conduct an internet search for factors that contribute to happiness in the workplace, compensation would most likely not be the leading contributor. I will explain how I learned this.

Over the years, my job as a provider grew increasingly demanding with long hours and ever-expanding responsibilities. As the tenured provider in the clinic, I was relied on heavily for everything from patient care to IT issues.

As my expected role expanded with the addition of more and more tasks, my compensation also increased which I viewed as a reflection of my value to the organization. However, even though I was being compensated at the high-end of the pay scale for my position, I did not feel happy or satisfied at work. Instead, I felt fatigued and weighed down by the extra responsibilities I had acquired. I was no longer excited to do my job and I found I was no longer invested or engaged in my work, rather I was mainly focused on just getting through the day. Finding enjoyment and ways to become engaged in my workplace were not priorities. Nor was this important to my organization as the only form of communication I had with my leaders always focused on the quantity of patients I saw.

Workplace satisfaction and employee fulfillment were also not priorities for my employer. All that seemed to matter to the organization was the number of patients being seen each day, and as the number of patient visits increased, so did my compensation and monthly bonus. At the time, I wrongly assumed that increased compensation was the driving force behind creating happy, engaged, and successful providers. On the contrary, as I continued to see high volumes of patients and earn more money, my level of contentment and fulfillment only worsened.

My own workplace satisfaction and fulfillment remained low until I had the opportunity to become involved in projects with initiatives that I was personally interested in (for me it was the performance improvement process).

I found myself re-engaged, and rather than dreading the day, I was excited to go to work. Suddenly, I went from constantly looking for happiness through tirelessly seeing more and more patients and increasing my compensation, to doing something I felt was meaningful and impactful on a much larger scale.

So, how does an organization determine what is meaningful to its providers to get them engaged and excited to come to work. Easy, you just have to ask.

STRATEGY 1: FIND OUT WHAT MATTERS THROUGH PROVIDER SURVEYS

Before the organization can expect engagement from providers, it must first assess what is meaningful to them. This can be accomplished through provider surveys. Organizations that conduct surveys with their providers, convey that their providers' opinions are important and appreciated. It also communicates to providers that their voice is being heard by an organization that is invested in what matters to them.

Exhibit 5.1: Provider Survey Questions

1. What has the greatest impact on your satisfaction at work?
   a. Paid time off
   b. Working with colleagues
   c. Workload
   d. Compensation
   e. Being involved in decision making
2. What do you enjoy about your job?
3. What is one thing you would change about your job?
4. Any additional comments?

Exhibit 5.1 is an example of the provider survey questions than can be used.

Effective questions should prompt providers to remember why they chose the medical profession and prompt them to think about what they enjoy about their job while also providing the opportunity to express what is important to them in the workplace.

> Organizations that conduct surveys with their providers, convey that their providers' opinions are important and appreciated.

The last open-ended question allows providers the opportunity to offer additional information and gives the organization a chance to see if there are common concerns or themes that the organization should be aware of and/or address.

Results to Anticipate

Organizations might assume that all providers prioritize compensation and time off. Under this assumption, organizations tend to reward providers with increased compensation, bonuses, and increased paid time off for job performance or tenure with the company.

Organizations should not be surprised to find that workload has a great impact on provider satisfaction. Across all fields, providers commonly express that they are overworked. This awareness can help the organization understand where to focus their attention to help their provider satisfaction rates. When providers can barely get through their day-to-day tasks, organizations cannot expect them to embrace or engage in new efforts, ideas, or goals.

> When providers can barely get through their day-to-day tasks, organizations cannot expect them to embrace or engage in new efforts, ideas, or goals.

Without insight from these surveys, organizations will continue to increase provider compensation to promote provider satisfaction and not focus on what really matters to providers. Organizations that continue in this dysfunctional cycle perpetuate provider turnover.

Provider Retention Efforts

Once surveys are conducted, the organization should strive to utilize this information and work to implement processes aimed at provider retention. This can be done through a work group comprised of various providers. Who better to tackle provider satisfaction and retention than providers themselves? This also gives them the opportunity to have their voices heard and make needed changes to improve their own work satisfaction. It is important for people to feel they are represented in the development processes that will directly affect them.

It is not enough to conduct provider surveys once; follow-up surveys should be completed, once new tools and processes have been implemented, to gather direct feedback on their effectiveness and ideas for further improvements.

Sustaining Provider Satisfaction and Retention

Determining what is needed for provider retention is simply not enough. Sustaining high provider satisfaction and retention rates is the ultimate goal. This is an evolving aspect of healthcare that requires constantly circling back to reassess provider satisfaction. We all know this can change from day to day as new issues and barriers arise.

To effectively do this, managers should conduct frequent check-ins with providers to keep a pulse on their level of satisfaction. Constant communication between the manager and leadership helps to keep leadership informed.

Routine provider surveys should also be done annually to ascertain how providers feel. Constant feedback is key for the organization to maintain open lines of communication with the providers and ensure providers feel heard and valued by their organization.

STRATEGY 2: OFFER A PLATFORM FOR COMRADERY THROUGH PROVIDER MEETINGS

It is not uncommon for providers to feel a lack of communication from leadership. A great way to rectify this is through routine provider meetings. These meetings offer a platform for collegial interactions and provide a bridge to close the gap between leadership and providers.

Provider meetings are an effective way to keep providers involved (e.g., in day-to-day operations, administrative duties, big-picture ideas) and to create opportunities for engagement with each other. These meetings offer the providers a platform to come together with peers to discuss a variety of topics and feel more connected. During these meetings, attendees can voice concerns, share best practices, and receive updates on big picture topics from the organization so they feel included.

Exhibit 5.2 show the benefits of routine provider meetings.

Ideally, provider meetings are conducted on a monthly basis with a small group. Meeting in smaller groups allows providers to get to know each other better and provides a more comfortable setting for them to voice thoughts and opinions. As a result, providers are much more engaged. It is also important for organizational leaders to attend these meetings to give providers a chance to express concerns and communicate needs.

Exhibit 5.3 is the typical agenda for provider meetings.

Additionally, an in-service is offered based on the topic or theme of the meeting. For instance, if blood pressure metrics are being discussed, then an in-service on blood pressure should be given. Ideally, the provider with the best performance in this metric will lead the in-service, since a provider who is working in the same capacity and treating the same population of patients as the rest of the group is

---

Exhibit 5.2: Benefits of Routine Provider Meetings

- Opportunity to interact with peers.
- Bridge the gap between providers and leadership.
- Stay informed on operational activities.
- Receive updates on various committees.
- Discuss quality measures and performance improvement goals.
- Share best practices across providers.
- Learn about opportunities for engagement.
- Feel a sense of camaraderie.

Exhibit 5.3: Provider Meeting Agenda

1. Welcome
2. Updates
3. Metrics
4. Educational in-service
5. Open Forum

---

the ideal person to provide guidance and insight on best practices. This is also an excellent opportunity to engage your top performing providers.

The meeting concludes with an open forum, giving the providers the opportunity to ask questions, provide comments, and engage in robust discussion.

STRATEGY 3: MAKE LEADERSHIP ACCESSIBLE

Provider meetings are an excellent way to bridge the gap between providers and leadership. They also give providers a platform to be heard by the organization.

Information from leadership can be disseminated through these meetings as well. Each time the organization deploys new initiatives, the rationale should be communicated to providers in order to get the buy-in and engagement necessary for successful implementation. Having a meeting between leadership and providers allows for these important discussions.

The "Why"

Leaders can engage providers by explaining "why" things should be done rather than directing "how" things should be done. It is important for leaders to communicate the meaning and purpose behind the organization's decisions and actions. Good leaders can gain provider buy-in with the "why" by focusing on the value created by their efforts.

> Leaders can engage providers by explaining "why" things should be done rather than directing "how" things should be done.

Leaders must recognize that provider engagement cannot be achieved through rules, regulations, and criticisms. Instead, they should give providers the reasoning behind strategies to improve performance and enhance patient outcomes. When providers understand the value of a process, they are more likely to accept and implement it. See chapter 1 for more information on managing change.

Knowing the Organizational Chart

Providers should also be made aware of the chain of command, including clinical and administrative leadership, with an organizational chart. This can also be reviewed during the provider meetings. Providers must know the most appropriate person to whom they can voice concerns and who can provide the solutions and answers they seek.

Failure to explain this structure leads to frustration and creates the illusion that no one is available to hear and address concerns.

STRATEGY 4: TAP INTO FRIENDLY COMPETITION THROUGH PROVIDER SCORECARDS

Constant communication and discussions surrounding metrics help improve provider engagement by bringing awareness to quality standards. These discussions also make the organization's expectations clear to the providers while promoting a natural competitive spirit among them.

Using Provider Scorecards

Many organizations have instituted provider scorecards to measure the various metrics the organization has deemed important. These can be sent directly to providers with the organization's goals and current provider metrics. Exhibit 5.4 is an example of a provider scorecard with the organization's goals for the diabetes metrics identified by HEDIS (Healthcare Effectiveness Data and Information Set; see chapter 8 for more information).

The Effect of Scorecards

Scorecards can help providers track their progress and identify areas for improvement. From an organizational standpoint, the scorecards provide a monitoring system to ensure interventions are initiated in a timely manner for those providers who may need help managing below-goal metrics. Scorecards can also validate the high-quality care providers are administering to their patients.

Exhibit 5.4: Sample Provider Scorecard

Provider Name:		
Metric	Goal	Score
HbA1c testing		
HbA1c poor control (>9.0%)		
HbA1c control (<8.0%)		
HbA1c control (<7.0%) for a selected population		
Eye exam (retinal) performed		
Medical attention for nephropathy		
BP control (<140/90 mmHg)		

Note: BP = blood pressure.

Competition Among Peers

The organization can take scorecards a step further by reporting their metrics to all the providers so they can see how they rate against one other. Each provider is assigned a private ID number known only to them. After the scorecards are distributed, the organization sends an email to all providers listing the scores for each ID. Exhibit 5.5 shows example provider metrics for HEDIS diabetes scores.

> Many organizations will see their metrics improve simply by showing providers how they rate against their peers.

Besides HbA1C, this system can be used successfully for several other metrics (e.g., blood pressure, statin use, kidney screening). Many organizations will see their metrics improve simply by showing providers how they rate against their peers.

Turn Patient Data into Meaningful Information

Once an organization chooses to initiate scorecards, it can expect to have some providers express their discontent or surprise with low scores, as many providers assume their metrics are good. On the other hand, scorecards can make providers aware of how well they are managing their chronic patients. Some providers may realize they would benefit from educational updates on chronic disease management or prescribing techniques. This can be an eye-opening moment that motivates providers to improve their practices and inspires them to help each other, all of which benefits patients.

Recruit High-Performing Providers

Scorecards also give the organization insight into who the highest performers are. These high performers should be given the opportunity to coach and educate

Exhibit 5.5: Provider Metrics for HEDIS Diabetes Scores

Provider Diabetes Scores for January Goal: 90% completion of HbA1c testing in patients with diabetes	
Provider ID	**HbA1c Completion Rate (%)**
111	72
GGT	80
667	96
XT2	65
RST	94
237	76
HDT	83

other providers on their process for successful patient management. For example, the highest-performing provider for blood pressure metrics can provide an in-service on how to properly treat blood pressure, which can easily be done during one of the provider meetings.

Recruiting high-performing providers in this way makes them feel appreciated by the organization. It validates their hard work and reassures them that their employer recognizes it. When providers are asked to help their colleagues by sharing their best practices, they feel a renewed sense of pride in their work, and their level of engagement deepens.

STRATEGY 5: OFFER OPPORTUNITIES FOR GROWTH

While I was attending a diabetes conference with a colleague, she expressed interest in helping her patients with diabetes through shared medical appointments (SMAs; see chapters 2 and 3 for more information). She was concerned about diabetes disproportionally affecting her patient population and wanted to start a group appointment targeting this specific cohort. Her worry was that the physician she worked for would not be interested in offering this at his private practice. The passion she had for this project was palpable, so I encouraged her to propose the idea to the physician.

I reconnected with her a few months later and was pleased to hear the excitement in her voice when she told me she had started offering SMAs at the private practice. When she proposed the concept of SMAs to the physician, he had never heard of it but was willing to let her trial it. My colleague was so excited to report the positive impact she was already seeing on their patients' diabetes in such a short amount of time. She felt a sense of accomplishment and growth in her career.

Empower Forward Thinkers

Organizations should give providers the opportunity to express their opinions and voice their ideas to improve patient care; this leads to more invested and involved providers and, in turn, to higher patient satisfaction. Providers should not simply be employed to crank out a high volume of patients. They should be encouraged to come up with "big picture" ideas.

> Organizations should give providers the opportunity to express their opinions and voice their ideas to improve patient care; this leads to more invested and involved providers and, in turn, to higher patient satisfaction.

Encourage Participation in Committees

Encouraging committee involvement fosters a sense of connection to the bigger picture. Committees afford providers the chance to be a part of the organization's progress. Rather than being implementers, they can be innovators. Who better to forge the path for process improvement and change than our frontline providers?

Coaching Providers for Successful Leadership

When providers lead committees, they can win greater buy-in from other providers. The providers can successfully lead change and garner engagement from their peers when they are set up for success. However, the organization should not expect providers, who are clinically driven, to automatically know how to lead and guide a committee. They must be coached.

A useful tool for coaching providers is the Tuckman model, which represents the different stages a team must go through in order to grow and become productive (Wageningen University and Research 2012). The purpose of the tool is to foster effective group cooperation through self-evaluation. It should be used during the co-creation stage, when the focus shifts toward developing group outputs. Tuckman's five stages of development can be applied to the establishment of a committee to help guide its success:

1. **Forming:** Members come together to get to know one another and establish goals. A clear leader who can direct the team should be determined.
2. **Storming:** Members brainstorm and the leader moves to a coaching role. Tasks are created and delegated to the members under the leader's guidance.
3. **Norming:** The team develops a strong sense of identity. Members have strong discussions about shared issues and begin to provide solutions.
4. **Performing:** In the team's final task, providers work cohesively to achieve their goals as the leader moves into a role of delegating.
5. **Adjourning:** The is the phase of celebration when the team has successfully achieved their goals.

To move through these stages seamlessly, the team must communicate, work together, have clarity of roles, and understand the goals. All team members must understand the value and meaning behind their purpose. The organization must help team leaders find solutions and implement change.

Steering Committee

This type of committee is becoming increasingly popular. Also known as a quality council, it can be composed of various members of the healthcare organization. This is the perfect committee to get providers involved as it focuses on establishing quality efforts, developing goals, creating a teamwork environment, developing policies, and creating systems such as rewards and recognition. Steering committees are excellent venues for providers to connect change with meaning and get involved at a higher level.

> **Steering committees are excellent venues for providers to connect change with meaning and get involved at a higher level.**

Connecting Meaning to Work

Organizations must provide meaningful opportunities for providers to grow and connect to their work. We all got into the business of healthcare for similar reasons, but we sometimes forget these reasons when we are focused on getting through day-to-day tasks. Create moments that prompt your providers to remember why they got into healthcare.

STRATEGY 6: PROTECT AGAINST BURNOUT

Provider burnout is known to be linked to poor quality outcomes, higher rates of malpractice, patient and provider turnover, low patient satisfaction scores, and poor health outcomes for providers (Drummond 2015). If providers are burned out, the first five strategies will be futile. Provider well-being must be safeguarded to meaningfully implement strategies designed to engage them.

> Provider well-being must be safeguarded to meaningfully implement strategies designed to engage them.

To protect against burnout, we must first understand what causes it. Over the years, several studies have been conducted to determine what causes burnout. From my personal experience as a provider who has burned out, here are what I believe to be its greatest causes:

- **Emotional stress:** This is an emotionally charged job. Every day we deal with sick, stressed, scared, and dying patients. They come to us to discuss their problems and frustrations. They tell us their most personal fears and concerns. The worst part of the job is giving bad news that can turn a patient's life upside down.
- **Not enough time:** There is simply not enough time to deal with emotional stress, growing patient demands, and the organization's expectations.

Most providers find joy in the time spent with their patients, but this time is shrinking because of the increasing administrative tasks placed on providers.

- **Provider shortage:** This is a large contributor to burnout, and the logistics are rarely discussed. When providers depart, those who remain are expected to carry the remaining workload. Leadership rarely discusses this with providers left behind—it is just assumed. As providers, we do not even question the additional workload, as our priority is taking care of patients. This contributed more to my burnout than any other factor, as I endured many years of continual provider turnover.

After considering the contributors to provider burnout, the organization must be able to identify when it is occurring. The burnout process can take a long time, making it difficult to recognize.

The American Academy of Family Physicians describes the Three Cardinal Symptoms of Burnout (Drummond 2015):

1. **Exhaustion:** The physician's physical and emotional energy levels are extremely low and spiraling downward. A common thought process at this point is, "I'm not sure how much longer I can keep this going."
2. **Depersonalization:** Also known as "compassion fatigue," this is signaled by cynicism, sarcasm, and the need to vent about your patients or your job. At this stage, you are not emotionally available for your patients, or anyone else for that matter. Your emotional energy is tapped dry.
3. **Lack of efficacy:** You begin to doubt the meaning and quality of your work and think, "What's the use? My work doesn't really serve a purpose anyway." You worry that you will make a mistake if things don't get better soon.

Now that we have identified what can cause burnout and how to identify it, let's discuss interventions. You can easily find many articles that offer solutions. They all recommend work–life balance, a reliable electronic health record, decreased administrative duties, and offering provider more paid time off. Truthfully, these are not always feasible for the organization to achieve.

As a provider who once went through burnout, I offer the following actions that I have found to be beneficial for managers:

- **Check in with the provider:** This is such a simple action, yet few managers do it. Checking in frequently with the provider lets them know the organization is concerned about their staff's well-being. It shows that leadership cares and is keeping the provider's welfare in mind. This is especially important when a provider is asked to take on additional duties, beyond the expectation of their role, to help with patient management.

- **Make time for mindfulness:** Offering time devoted to mindfulness can help with stress management. Just ten minutes of uninterrupted time per day can reset the provider and help reduce their anxiety. The organization may think of revenue loss when a patient is not seen during these ten minutes, but the benefits of a refreshed provider far outweigh this loss. Providers need this dedicated time. Go beyond just recommending it to your providers; urge them to schedule and protect it. Mindfulness breaks also can take the form of administrative time when patients are not scheduled.
- **Ask providers for solutions:** Providers are frequently thought of as solution implementers. Leadership and administrators analyze issues, create solutions, and rely on the providers to execute. When looking at provider burnout, the organization needs to make providers part of the analysis process by asking them directly, "What is causing you to burnout?" This answer may be different for individual providers, but by asking each one, solutions can be tailored.

The "Don't" List
- Don't wait until providers burn out to get them engaged. Start the engagement process early.
- Don't set goals for the providers. Give them a voice in setting goals meaningful to them.
- Don't forget to communicate.
- Don't permit toxic behaviors or processes.
- Don't focus on quantity of visits over quality.

MY STORY

When I first started working as a primary care provider, I was fresh, excited, and willing to soak up everything I possibly could like a sponge. After I felt well established in this setting and was having a positive impact on patients, I started to think about ways we could improve processes and work more efficiently. I was excited to share my ideas with our director and even more excited to aid our staff.

Once I finally had an audience with my supervisor, which was difficult to get, I was incredibly disheartened with the negative feedback I received. He was not interested in any of my ideas. I was essentially told my purpose was not to come up with ideas to improve the work environment; rather, I was paid to see patients.

I was shocked. At the time, I could not understand why anyone would not want to hear ideas on how to improve staff and patient experience.

This was the moment that I realized my supervisor was not interested in what I had to say, which I felt was a reflection of the organization. It only saw me as a means to make them money through seeing patients. My value was simply measured by the number of patients I saw, not the level of care I provided or any of the process improvement ideas I could develop. I quickly learned this was not the type of organization I wanted to work for.

Soon after this realization, I tendered my resignation. I was quickly offered more money, which prompted me to stay, but I was still unhappy. My heart was not in it. The extra money was great, but I had zero job satisfaction. Truthfully, what I really wanted was to be heard, valued, and engaged.

It was not until I started working for another organization that valued me, listened to my ideas, and allowed me to become more engaged that I began to feel satisfied with my job.

The satisfaction grew further when I started getting involved in performance improvement projects, specifically with piloting shared medical appointments. Chapter 3 details all the benefits of SMAs for patients, but for me personally, this is where I found my passion for process improvement.

Without the patient-centered medical home (PCMH) model, I would not have learned about SMAs, nor would I have been given the opportunity to pilot this type of patient visit. I am thankful that my organization transitioned to the PCMH model, which suddenly opened the door for multiple process-improvement opportunities.

PCMHS FOR PROVIDER MORALE AND JOB SATISFACTION THROUGH QUALITY IMPROVEMENT

> When providers are given opportunities for involvement in quality improvement, the organization will achieve greater levels of engagement, higher morale, and better work productivity.

A well-run organization that uses the PCMH model will find opportunities to involve providers through quality improvement. This model places a constant focus on quality improvement in the continuously changing healthcare field. Providers should be pulled in to have a voice in this process. When providers are given opportunities for involvement in quality improvement, the organization will achieve greater levels of engagement, higher morale, and better work productivity.

A study was conducted to determine the effects of the PCMH on staff satisfaction, morale, and burnout rates (Lewis et al. 2012). Researchers measured the staff's perceptions of the PCMH on five subscales. Of these subscales, providers and staff responded most positively to the quality improvement aspect of the PCMH. "Among the PCMH subscales, the quality improvement subscale score particularly correlated with higher morale, greater job satisfaction, and freedom from burnout" (p. 23). The study also reported that "physicians whose practices engaged in quality improvement efforts noted significantly less isolation, stress, and dissatisfaction with their work" (p. 24).

Improving quality and process improvement is how to get providers' attention. Providers want to work for organizations that value these initiatives. This is why we got into the business of healthcare in the first place: to improve the quality of our patients' lives.

How Provider Engagement Affects Patient Experience

Provider engagement is known to positively affect patient experience. Providers who are invested in quality outcomes and in their patients tend to have better patient outcomes and engagement. Relevant to the organization, this affects patient loyalty and revenue as patients are likely to return and refer friends and family.

> Providers who are invested in quality outcomes and in their patients tend to have better patient outcomes and engagement.

To gauge provider engagement, patient experience surveys can be tailored to determine the level of engagement patients perceive from their providers. Exhibit 5.6 is an example of survey questions that can determine patients' perceptions.

Press Ganey Surveys

Another way to assess patient satisfaction and their perceptions of providers is through Press Ganey surveys. Press Ganey's mission has been to support healthcare

---

Exhibit 5.6: Survey Questions to Gauge Patient-Perceived Provider Engagement

1. Did your provider ask you about stressors?
2. Did your provider ask you if you have the tools needed to manage your disease?
3. Did your provider ask you about your SMART goals (see chapter 3)?
4. Did your provider ask you about barriers to achieving your health goals?
5. Did your provider give you options for your treatment plan?
6. Does your provider know what is important to you?

---

providers in understanding and improving care delivery to transform the patient experience. In 2021, Press Ganey received approval from the Centers for Medicare & Medicaid Services to administer the Primary Care First Patient Experience of Care Survey (Press Ganey 2021), which allows consumers to rate their provider experience. The results are then made available to potential consumers.

How to Get Providers to Improve Patient Satisfaction Scores

Engaged providers are more likely to receive higher ratings. Accordingly, negative patient provider feedback can be a sensitive subject. No provider enjoys learning of a poor rating. Yet rather than addressing this, organizations tend to give providers the information without discussing with them how to improve their performance.

What if the organization took a different approach? Rather than focusing on past scores, ask the providers for ideas on how to improve future scores. Another good idea is to show providers the patient survey questions so they know how they are being graded and on what. Providers can then tailor their patient interactions to these questions. For instance, if a provider knows the patient survey specifically asks, "Did your provider ask if you had any medication questions?" the provider can ensure they ask every patient this exact question. When the patient is then surveyed, they will remember being asked this and respond positively.

Providers need to be part of the process and the solution.

What Patients Are Looking For

In today's healthcare market, patients are shopping for providers and organizations they can partner with. They want to be an integral part of the decision-making process. See chapters 2 and 3 for more information on patient-centered care.

They do not want providers entering each visit with a quickly executed, predetermined agenda. Patients are looking for a conversation and partnership with their providers to help establish and achieve their own healthcare goals, not the provider's. This relationship is fostered by asking the questions in exhibit 5.6, making eye contact, listening, giving patients options, and taking the time to cultivate a connection. This can only occur when providers are engaged in their patients and with their organization. For an organization to optimize this patient experience, they must invest in their providers and set them up for success.

KEY POINTS

- The PCMH model offers the ideal setting for provider engagement.
- Survey providers to determine what is meaningful to them.

- Provider meetings help with communication and bridging the gap between providers and leadership.
- Tap into friendly competition.
- Foster growth opportunities through committee involvement and ingenuity.
- Gain a sense of the patient's perception of provider engagement using patient satisfaction surveys.

REFERENCES

Drummond, D. 2015. "Physician Burnout: Its Origin, Symptoms, and Five Main Causes." *Family Practice Management Journal* 22 (5): 42–47.

Lewis, S., R. Nocon, H. Tang, S. Park, A. Vable, L. Casalino, E. Huang, M. Quinn, D. Burnet, W. Summerfelt, J. Birnberg, and M. Chin. 2012. "Patient-Centered Medical Home Characteristics and Staff Morale in Safety Net Clinics." *Journal of the American Medical Association* 172 (1): 23–31.

Press Ganey. 2021. "Press Ganey Receives CMS Approval to Administer Primary Care First Patient Experience of Care Surveys." Published June 3. http://about. pressganey.com/about/press-releases/press-release-details/2021/Press-Ganey-Receives-CMS-Approval-to-Administer-Primary-Care-First-Patient-Experience-of-Care-Surveys/default.aspx.

Wageningen University and Research. 2012. "Tuckman (Forming, Norming, Storming, Performing)." www.mspguide.org/tool/tuckman-forming-norming-storming-performing.

CHAPTER 6

Patient and Family Engagement

Let's start with another one of my (Mary-Ellen's) personal healthcare stories. I made an appointment with my primary care office to get medical clearance for another minor surgical procedure. My provider was not available on that day so I was scheduled with the nurse practitioner (NP).

Shortly after I arrived, the nurse called me in and proceeded to take my weight and other vitals. I thought her manner was rather brusque, but I did not remark on it.

As she brought me into the exam room, she apologized for not being more chipper, explaining that she had a headache caused by fumes from a fire in the microwave earlier that day. She went on to tell me that she thought the employee who caused the fire should be terminated. In addition, she complained about patients who came in on Friday with a cold of two days' duration and expected to get antibiotics.

She left to get the ECG machine. The NP entered a short time later. She started taking my history and conducting the necessary examination. I mentioned that I had two small bumps on my finger. She looked at them quickly and stated that she would get back to those after the physical exam was complete. She did, and, suggested that they might be bites. I responded that I had Googled my symptoms, but she cut me off with the statement, "I don't believe in Google!"

This gave me pause, but I went on to say that I had a history of cysts. She responded, "There is nothing in your record about cysts." I would venture to say that not every aspect of my medical history is collected in any one medical record.

She then indicated that she would hold off on my medical clearance to make sure that I didn't have an infection. She left the room.

I waited quite some time for the nurse to return with the ECG machine. When she did, she said that she had gotten involved in an emergency that was not a true emergency. I shared with her that my visit was not going well, telling her how I felt dismissed by the NP regarding the bumps on my fingers when I mentioned that I had Googled my symptoms. The nurse responded, "Don't Google!"

I was taken aback once again. This felt very much like the old, one-way medical model, certainly not patient friendly in an era that now encourages patients to partner in their healthcare. She continued, "In all fairness, she is the only one here today and she is constantly running." This did not comfort me.

Having completed the ECG, the nurse left the exam room. When the NP returned, I sensed a change in her demeanor. She was more open to a two-way dialogue. I assumed that the nurse had conveyed my concerns.

Nothing about this visit made me feel cared for. Clearly I was not at the center of the encounter. I was made to feel that I was an annoyance, just another patient for staff to deal with so they could get through their busy day.

How do we avoid interactions such as this one? In this chapter we will identify and discuss strategies for engaging patients and their family members to ensure an optimal experience.

DEFINING PATIENT AND FAMILY ENGAGEMENT

Frampton et al. (2017, 1) define patient- and family-engaged care as "planned, delivered, managed, and continuously improved in active partnership with patients and their families [. . .] to ensure integration of their health and healthcare goals, preferences, and values. It includes explicit and partnered determination of goals and care options, and it requires ongoing assessment of the care match with patient goals." Every aspect should be purposeful and carefully designed, monitored, and evaluated. Such planning should include continuous feedback loops that incorporate the voice of the customer, which goes beyond the patient to include and embrace family and friends—anyone involved in and supporting the patient's care.

The old medical model focused on changing patients' behaviors. Patients were seen as a problem to be fixed. Compliance was the goal. It's time to change the culture to one that continuously integrates patient and family perspectives. Their involvement should be valued when designing systems and processes at the point of care and across the healthcare organization. Likewise, multidirectional communication is a critical success factor. We need to encourage patients to participate in their care and tell them how they can make a difference.

ENGAGEMENT AND THE POPULATION HEALTH MODEL

Let's talk about population health as an engagement strategy. As mentioned in chapter 1, the goal of population health management is to improve care, treatment, and outcomes for major consumers of healthcare resources—5 percent of the patient population with a chronic disease diagnosis uses 50 percent of these resources (Cohen 2014).

This model is a proactive approach that promotes healthy lifestyles while factoring in the social determinants of health (SDOH). Successful models require the engagement of the whole team, including providers, stakeholders, and the community. Equity of access is the goal, and pursuing it starts with a focus on the physical and mental health of patient populations, along with their social and spiritual well-being.

Community health assessments, required by the Affordable Care Act and Centers for Medicare & Medicaid Services, help to identify both the needs and the gaps in community resources and programs. They give us a more expansive view of the patient population over and above clinical information. Assessment parameters include the following:

- Access to behavioral health and dental care
- Multigenerational care
- Peer–peer support
- Parenting
- Transportation
- Economic opportunity
- Inclusion of men in family health decision making
- Safety and violence prevention
- Access to healthy food

To provide a full complement of services and options to address healthcare needs, it truly takes a whole village: faith-based organizations, advocacy groups, cultural institutions, the criminal justice system, city and county agencies—and let's not forget healthcare organizations.

Communities are able to partner and get creative to develop solutions. Here is a short list of actions to fill gaps in healthcare needs:

- Renovating public housing to help with asthma control
- Farmers' markets and "veggie-mobiles" in food deserts
- Supermarket teaching kitchens

- Transit planning
- Employment counseling
- School programs to increase students' physical activity, prevent violence, and identify safe routes to schools
- Community-based education programs on risk reduction (e.g., motorcycle injury prevention, tobacco cessation)
- Access to clean syringes
- Pricing strategies for alcohol products

Employers are also getting involved by focusing on preventing obesity. Stairwells with inspiring posters and piped-in music, fitness centers, and walkable grounds encourage patients and visitors—and staff—to be active.

Patient Activation Measure

Some organizations have invested in a chief population health officer to lead such efforts, and use the patient activation measure (PAM) to assess individual patient's level of engagement. The PAM measures the level of a patient's engagement, providing insight into their attitude, what motivates them, and their behavior. As described by Greene et al. (2015), patients at Level 1, who lack confidence to participate in their healthcare and look to their doctor to take the lead, account for 10 to 15 percent of the population. Level 2 contains patients who are becoming engaged in their care but still have a way to go. At Level 3, patients are becoming members of the team, building skills and identifying goals. Patients at Level 4 are focused on a healthy lifestyle; they act as their own advocate.

Exhibit 6.1 summarizes and breaks down the patient population by level of engagement.

Social Determinants of Health

SDOH are a community's vital signs, which identify at-risk populations from various social issues: What is the patient's economic situation? Stable, unable to pay routine bills, overwhelmed with debt? What about their living situation—is it clean and safe? Does the patient have transportation to medical appointments? Do they have access to recreational activities, healthy food, and clean water? What is the patient's educational level? It is easy to see how these elements factor into patient engagement. Indeed, they account for 70 percent of health outcomes. To improve patient and community health, we need to concentrate on the nonmedical factors that affect well-being.

Exhibit 6.1: The Four Levels of Patient Activation

Level (% of General Population)			
1 (10%–15%)	2 (20%–25%)	3 (25%–30%)	4 (20%–25%)
Predisposed to be passive	**Building knowledge and confidence**	**Taking action**	**Maintaining behaviors, pushing further**
Patients lack the confidence to play an active role in their health. *"My doctor is in charge of my health."*	Patients have some knowledge but gaps remain. They can set simple goals. *"I could be doing more."*	Patients have the key facts and are building skills. They are goal oriented. *"I'm part of my primary care team."*	Patients have adopted new behaviors but may struggle in times of stress or change. Healthy lifestyle is a key focus. *"I am my own advocate."*

Source: Adapted from Greene et al. (2015).

Well-being is defined as having opportunity, being happy, and experiencing no stress. Patients with high well-being are more likely to engage in healthy behaviors, develop social connections, and build strong support systems.

Exhibit 6.2 describes the key elements of the SDOH.

Exhibit 6.2: Social Determinants of Health

Economic Stability	Environment	Education	Food	Community Social Context	Healthcare System
Employment	Housing	Literacy	Hunger	Social education	Health coverage
Income	Transportation	Language	Access to healthy options	Support systems	Provider availability
Debt	Safety	Childhood education		Community engagement	Provider language
Medical bills	Parks	Vocational training		Discrimination	Provider cultural competency
Support	Playgrounds	Higher education			Quality of care

Source: Data from Office of Disease Prevention and Health Promotion (2020).

The following community-assessment-gap solutions that address specific SDOH can be added to the list in the "Engagement and the Population Health Model section:

- Relaxed traffic
- Walkable neighborhoods
- Mixed-use land
- Bike shares
- Rail trails

When a whole community comes together to raise the health status of its members, the options are endless.

How do individual clinics integrate the SDOH in their practices? Here are a few examples:

- Creating a Spanish-language video describing the benefits of colon cancer screening in a clinic serving a large Hispanic population
- Using cartoons as a way to initiate difficult conversations with victims of sexual trauma
- Language interpretation services
- Clothing and food drives to support patients in poorer areas
- Purposefully siting clinics on a bus route
- Providing integrative medicine options, such as yoga and tai chi, in remote areas through the use of technology
- Free parking

Whole Health

In 1948, the World Health Organization (2020) defined *health* as "a state of complete physical, mental and social well-being and not merely the absence of disease or infirmity." We have come full circle to appreciate that our patients are not simply a set of presenting symptoms to treat. They are unique individuals with unique stories.

To be effective healthcare partners, we need to know our patients' stories. What matters most to them? What are their goals for their healthcare? What are their preferences in how they receive care? These are all important questions to consider as we nurture the human being—body, mind, and spirit—beneath the diagnosis and look at our systems through their eyes.

Organizations are becoming increasingly sophisticated in their approaches to patient and family engagement. The Veterans Health Administration

(VHA; Bokhour et al. 2020) has developed a Whole Health model designed to create a strong partnership between the patient and the primary care team. The VHA defines *Whole Health* as "Personalized, Proactive, Patient-driven care, an approach to healthcare that empowers and equips people to take charge of their health and well-being and live life to the fullest." It takes us beyond the presenting symptoms to focus on the patient's values, aspirations and goals for well-being. Getting to know the patient's story, needs, and expectations of care is key.

> Getting to know the patient's story, needs, and expectations of care is key.

The primary care team's conversation with the patient includes a discussion of what matters most in the patient's life. Given these stated priorities, is the patient doing everything they can to achieve the goals? Together, the patient and the primary care team set goals and build the health plan to achieve those goals, identifying resources within the healthcare system and the community to support the plan. The use of appreciative inquiry to ask meaningful, open-ended questions helps the team understand the patient's needs in order to meet their goals.

The patient also completes a Personal Health Inventory, which becomes part of the medical record. As the patient progresses through this tool, they rate how they feel about their physical and mental/emotional well-being as well as their day-to-day life.

Next the patient describes their purpose. What do you live for? What matters most to you? They rate themselves on various aspects of self-care: moving the body, nutrition, personal development, spirituality, recharging, professional care, and more. The answers help the patient and primary care team formulate their healthcare goals with regard to these aspects:

- Movement and physical activities
- Sleep and relaxation
- Learning, work, and community involvement
- Relationships
- Spirituality and resilience
- Physical environment
- Mindfulness
- Healthcare and prevention

This approach provides fully integrated care, focused on the whole person. Partnership and shared responsibility, together with access to supportive resources, are the critical success factors. No longer is it enough to focus on and treat only the patient's complaints—indeed, that was never enough. We would wonder why

> Without engagement, without knowing the patient's story and expectations, treatment cannot succeed.

patients weren't compliant with their treatment plan. Without engagement, without knowing the patient's story and expectations, treatment cannot succeed.

Mindfulness

Fully integrated care, focused on the whole person, moves our expectation as healthcare providers from "patient compliance" to patient engagement. The Whole Health approach promotes mindfulness of the primary care team and the patient to improve the experience.

Training and mindfulness tools are available to staff, particularly those in high-stress areas and during high-stress events such as the COVID-19 pandemic. The aim is to optimize staff health, well-being, and performance while empowering patients to be more active in their health. (And of course, there's an app for that! Via their mobile devices, patients and staff can have mindfulness at their fingertips to use any time they need a short break.)

> Fully integrated care, focused on the whole person, moves our expectation as healthcare providers from "patient compliance" to patient engagement.

The VHA is using this mindfulness approach for patients with chronic pain, mental health conditions, and chronic disease diagnoses, including complementary and integrative health therapies such as health coaching, acupuncture, pain management groups, dietitian appointments, and a peer-led course aimed at goal creation. Early results are displayed in exhibit 6.3.

Patients and employees both appear to benefit from the implementation of a Whole Health approach to care; see exhibit 6.4.

Exhibit 6.3: Early Results of Efforts to Promote Veteran Mindfulness

- Greater improvements in the perceptions of the care received as being more person centered
- Greater improvements in engagement in healthcare and self-care
- Greater improvements in perceived stress, indicating improvement in overall well-being
- Reduction in opioid use
- Reduction in pharmacy costs

Source: Data from Bokhour et al. (2020).

Exhibit 6.4: Circle of Health: Me + Self-Care + Professional Care + Community

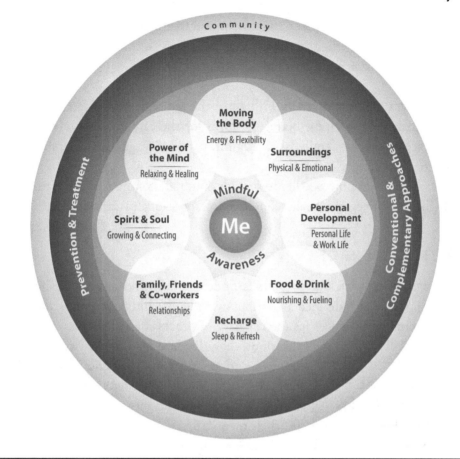

Source: Data from Bokhour et al. (2020).

CULTURAL COMPETENCE AND DIVERSITY

Do the composition of your staff and the nature of your care practices reflect those whom you serve? An analysis of your patient demographic will help identify the racial and ethnic cultures you need to consider when hiring staff and designing culturally competent services. The goal is to contribute to the elimination of racial and ethnic health disparities while improving health outcomes and quality of care.

What can you do to meet this goal? Here are a few approaches:

- Provide staff training on cultural competency and cross-cultural issues.

> The goal is to contribute to the elimination of racial and ethnic health disparities while improving health outcomes and quality of care.

- Include a diverse group of patients, reflecting your patient population, on your patient/family advisory council.
- Ensure, through the patient assessment and treatment processes, that patients' cultural, religious, or spiritual beliefs are accommodated.
- Mitigate language and communication barriers.

Understanding how diversity influences the patient's perception of their care and treatment will provide a better platform for the care process. Diversity goes beyond race to involve family, age, religion, nationality, gender, disability status, and socioeconomic backgrounds.

If we are not working together to provide culturally competent care, patients will be at higher risk of negative health consequences, poor-quality care, or dissatisfaction.

HEALTH LITERACY

Key to partnering with our patients is understanding and addressing health literacy. *Health literacy* is defined as reading, writing, listening, speaking, math skills, and conceptual knowledge. It's the capacity to process basic information to make decisions. Low literacy may affect patients' ability to read and understand instructions on medicine bottles, health educational materials, and insurance forms, and their competence to make decisions and set their own goals.

> Half of all American adults have difficulty understanding and using healthcare information.

Half of all American adults have difficulty understanding and using healthcare information (Office of Disease Prevention and Health Promotion 2020). I was surprised that this number was so high. In the face of illness and stress, even excellent readers may struggle with health information. Let's review some tools and strategies to address health literacy:

- Universal precautions, in this context, means always offering assistance. For example, at check-in, the medical assistant would ask the patient if they need help in filling out the forms.
- Teach-back is giving information and asking the patient to repeat it back.
- Chunk and Check is providing information in digestible chunks and checking understanding as you go.
- Language interpreting and translation services.

The primary care team should identify the patient's oral and written communication needs, including the patient's preferred language for discussing healthcare.

We should always use simple, understandable language and visuals to promote understanding.

Patient Education

Let's explore this topic further. Using the tools to address health literacy, every member of the patient-centered medical home team is part of the patient education process. Effective educators determine patients' needs, treat patients as individuals and partners, and offer clear explanations, using the following steps:

- **Assess:** Define needs, concerns, and readiness.
- **Plan:** Set learning objectives and identify materials.
- **Implement:** Execute the plan.
- **Document:** Ensure effective communication with the rest of the team.

Creating bridges between patients' needs and concerns through effective education can lead to realistic patient goals. Exhibit 6.5 illustrates this concept.

Don't forget to include family members and caregivers in the education process. They can act as invaluable supports to the treatment plan and the patient's goals.

Patient/Family Advisory Councils

Yet another approach to engaging our patients is the patient/family advisory council (PFAC), a formal group that meets regularly with leaders and staff to discuss and give input on policy and program decisions. This is a great way to get the voice of the customer on topics such as new construction, the Patient's Handbook, food and parking—all usually areas of concern and complaints from our patients.

Exhibit 6.5: Example Bridges to Help Patients Set Goals

Patient Need	Patient Concern	Bridge
Healthy eating to manage cholesterol and diabetes	Not being able to eat favorite foods	Offer a nutrition consult and recipes for tasty meals.
Increasing movement through exercise	Thinking that all exercise hurts	Start slow with low-impact options.
Smoking cessation	It's hard to quit	Offer classes and support groups.

Here is an outline of the scope of the PFAC:

- Serves as a communication channel and improves relationships among patients, families, and staff
- Provides a way for patients and families to assist in evaluating and providing input on the delivery of patient services
- Collaborates in partnership with staff, providers, and leadership in the planning and operation of programs to enhance care and services
- Provides a forum for staff to listen to their customers
- Establishes a link between the healthcare organization and the community

Fifteen to twenty members, with an executive as champion, and a patient as a co-leader, make for a manageable group. Typical members include the patient advocate, a nursing representative, and the chaplain. Department heads and front-line staff can be members or make presentations on an ad hoc basis.

How do you identify your patient members? Through complaint letters, surveys, the patient advocate, and other staff. They often know good candidates.

I have recently heard of an organization that had difficulty getting members to the table because of busy schedules and driving distances. So, they hold virtual meetings and it works well for them.

Taking it a step further, some of these patients can also act as "advisors," conducting mystery shops, presenting at staff onboarding, serving on hospital committees, presenting their story at town hall meetings, and advocating for the organization in the community.

I know of an organization that invites a patient to address all new hires during onboarding. This patient shares his experiences at various healthcare facilities across the country: the good, the bad, and the ugly. He holds nothing back as he communicates his expectations for the staff.

Potential barriers to a successful PFAC include:

1. Leadership and culture that are top-down
2. Fear that patients' and their families' suggestions might be unreasonable
3. Concern about confidentiality
4. Lack of guidance and support

If these barriers are successfully mitigated through careful design and rollout, and respectful interactions, the PFAC presents a win-win for the patient and the healthcare organization. Patients and families gain a better understanding of the healthcare system, appreciate being listened to, understand how to become active participants in their care, and develop close relationships with other members on the council.

The PFAC provides a venue for receiving and responding to patient or family input, resulting in better-informed planning. It leads to increased understanding and partnerships among patients, families, and staff while transforming the culture toward patient-centered care.

See appendix H for a sample PFAC charter.

High Reliability Organization

We discussed the high-reliability organization framework for safety in chapter 4 as it related to staff engagement. What's in it for our patients? With zero preventable harm as the aim, systems and processes are designed, monitored, evaluated, and improved relentlessly to provide a safe environment for our patients.

We can include patients on process improvement teams and invite them to safety forums to share their stories. There is nothing like hearing directly from those who experience adverse events to get staff's attention. This direct conduit to the voice of the customer informs problem solving and solution creation.

In turn, our patients learn that we are committed to their safety and value their involvement in continuous process improvement. We take it to the next step by including a patient as a member on our quality council.

Full Disclosure

What happens when an adverse patient event occurs? How we handle these incidents can have a significant impact on the patient–provider–organization relationship. Transparency and inclusion are important. Informing the patient and the family about the incident, keeping them in the loop, and including them in the improvement process are key.

To inform patients and families of adverse events, acknowledge what happened, apologize, demonstrate empathy and concern, and improve processes to prevent further occurrences. Invite them to share their story at a town hall or safety forum. Openness sets the stage for reflection, learning, and continuous improvement.

Don't forget the staff during this time. They are often the second victims of an adverse event who need your support.

What are the ramifications of not being highly reliable?

- Increased costs of care and administration
- Increased external oversight
- Decreased reimbursement
- Decreased patient satisfaction
- Increased potential for healthcare-acquired conditions
- Time away from the core function

SUPPORTING THE CAREGIVER

> We must partner with patients' caregivers to create better health outcomes for our patients.

Let's widen the circle of patient experience by extending the concepts of Whole Health to patients' family and friends, who are often their caregivers. By providing support and completing health-related tasks between clinic visits, these caregivers can have a great impact on the patient's health and well-being. We must partner with them to create better health outcomes for our patients.

To begin with a look at the caregiver role, review this list of functions, which is comprehensive but not all-inclusive:

- Provide transportation to appointments
- Assist with patient goals
- Assist with activities of daily living
- Prepare meals and handle the shopping
- Remind patients to take medications
- Offer love and encouragement
- Act as advocate and liaison with the primary care team

This list indeed could go on. The point is that caregivers play a critical, irreplaceable role in the health of their loved ones.

So how do we take care of the caregivers? By connecting them to some of the same wellness activities that we provide to our patients. Caregivers do a superb job of taking care of others, often at the expense of their own well-being. Through self-care, caregivers can restore their energy, gather strength, and get a short respite from their responsibilities.

Many healthcare organizations have recognized the need to provide this support and have acted on it by creating resources to enhance caregiver well-being. The team social worker is often the go-to person for these supports. Exhibit 6.6 lists and describes approaches and tools for caregiver support.

Share these self-care tips with your patients' caregivers. Your staff can benefit from them as well.

- **Physical:** Take some time out of your day today to soak in a candlelit tub, get a haircut or massage, take a quiet walk, or relax with a cup of tea. Renew your body with some kindness and care and see how it changes your day.
- **Mental:** Wake up your mind by taking a risk, learning a new word, writing a poem, playing a memory game, or reading.

Exhibit 6.6: Approaches and Tools for Caregiver Support

Resource	Description
Self-care courses	Topics include "Taking Care of Yourself," "Managing Stress," "Utilizing Technology," "Problem Solving," and "Effective Communication"
Caregiver support line	Available to address immediate needs and provider education
Journaling	Daily self-care reflections as a means of connecting with one's well-being
Support groups and networks	Provide discussion platforms and the chance to share the lived experience while connecting with others who provide care to loved ones
Respite programs	Temporary relief to a primary caregiver from the continuous support and care of a family member
Peer mentoring	Provides guidance to caregivers through sharing experiences and skill building with other caregivers
Mental health counseling	Professional support for the caregiver
Wellness activities	Yoga, mindfulness, and breathing exercises
Self-care techniques	See "Self-Care Tips for Caregivers," this chapter

Source: Data from Bokhour et al. (2020).

- **Emotional:** Notice and name feelings; identify your unmet needs.
- **Behavioral:** Start a new, small habit or let go of an old one.
- **Social:** Reach out, write a letter, call a friend. Connection has the power to heal.
- **Nature:** Awaken the senses through bird watching, stargazing, or walking in the woods.
- **Visualization:** Listen to recordings to help visualize calm scenes and settings. Try guided-imagery exercises to help you relax.

Breathing exercises, healthy eating, physical exercise, and adequate sleep round out the list.

VOLUNTEERS

Let's not forget another important part of the care team: our volunteers. A valuable resource, volunteers support patients, families, and staff in the primary care setting. Careful screening, orientation, ongoing evaluation, and matching interests to opportunities ensure a good fit for both the organization and the volunteer. Volunteer duties include the following:

- Escorting patients
- Ensuring adequate supplies of wheelchairs at the clinic entrance as well as refreshments and reading materials in the waiting room
- Administrative tasks
- Providing and gathering information
- Participating in a pet therapy program (see chapter 7)
- Emotional support; just being there to listen

We need to be purposeful about nurturing and providing support and recognition to this group of dedicated caregivers.

IMPROVING PATIENT ACCESS

Patient feedback indicates that, in addition to caring relationships with the primary care team, patients value timely access to all aspects of their care.

Enhancing Access to Care

Enhanced access allows patients and families more flexibility to attend appointments. Same-day appointments, expanded hours (including evenings and weekends), 24-hour coverage, and telehealth are becoming commonplace in the primary care space. Acting as the hub of the patient's healthcare experience, the primary care provider facilitates access to acute care, oral health services, urgent and emergent care, preventive services, rehabilitative equipment, substance abuse treatment, eye care and behavioral health needs. Coordination of these transitions ensures the continuity of care.

Enhancing Access to Information

Critical to engaging our patients is ensuring that they have access to the information that they need to be an active partner in their healthcare. Here's what doesn't work: filing a request with the medical records department, paying a fee, waiting days or even weeks to have your request filled. Then you may receive a CD that you can't access or you are forced to review your record with the clerk looking over your shoulder.

Now let's talk about what does work. Enter the open notes movement, initiated by Thomas Delbanco, MD, in 2010. This experiment provided secure portals for patients to read their medical records and enter notes of their own.

Patients became better educated about and more engaged in their care, and even identified errors. Their family members and caregivers also became more engaged (Delbanco 2016).

Although open notes aren't for everyone, two out of three patients liked reading their physician's notes. They felt that they could better remember instructions they were given during their office visit or at discharge. They had quicker access to their test results and appreciated the opportunity to help improve the accuracy of the record. A year after initiating the practice, not one physician stopped sharing notes. Full transparency promotes better provider–patient partnership.

The Role of Technology

In chapters 2 and 3 we discussed the use of telehealth and telemedicine to provide patients remote access to services. These strategies are becoming more commonplace as the COVID-19 pandemic catalyzes change. Our patients are acclimating to these tools and, indeed, have come to expect them in the primary care space.

Many healthcare organizations leveraged apps and social media during the pandemic to remain connected to patients, who then became aware of such resources for mental and physical health. The VHA (Bokhour et al. 2020) disseminated 16,000 laptops and more than 7,500 phones to veterans in rural areas as a means of continuing healthcare, especially mental health services. Similarly, when community clinics and practices were forced to shut their doors to routine care at the onset of the pandemic, telehealth became the means for providers and patients to stay connected. As COVID-19 surged, so did the number of telehealth visits. The result: Telehealth is here to stay.

The challenge lies in nurturing the patient–provider relationship via this platform to ensure that the patient feels cared for and heard. Patients report that their providers are more focused on them as clinicians leverage their communication skills to overcome the loss of subtle body language cues. The unexpected benefit to providers of seeing inside patients' homes gives them insight into living conditions and helps them offer in-home supports.

Exhibit 6.7 displays an array of telehealth services.

Taking full advantage of these technology-based solutions can increase patient engagement and partnership while meeting the needs of older, sicker, and poorer populations. Addressing their needs with telehealth is the core of a successful population health strategy.

As we design these services, we need to include the patient and their family members so we can understand the impact and the challenges inherent in new technology. This would be a good topic for your PFAC: How do technology-driven services affect the consumer experience?

Exhibit 6.7: Telehealth Services

- Remote monitoring of vital signs
- Remote provider–patient consultations
- Access to specialty services: dermatology, cardiology, behavioral health
- Retinal exams
- Yoga and tai chi classes
- Life coaching
- Social work support
- Nutrition class
- Disease-specific educational services
- Access to patient records for test results, scheduling appointments, and communicating with the primary care team

---

Secure patient portals provide access to test results, medication refills, appointments, education, and communication with the primary care team. Additionally, the VHA (Bokhour et al. 2020) has created "Annie," a text-messaging service that promotes self-care for patients and caregivers. Annie texts stress-management tips to caregivers three times per week. Messages may be educational or motivational, or may describe a stress-management activity.

ANOTHER PATIENT ENGAGEMENT STORY

Let me finish this chapter with another story—Mrs. Rooney's story.

Mrs. Rooney is 62 years old, has heart failure and diabetes, and recently moved to a new town to be near her daughter. She calls a local doctor's office to make an appointment. The scheduler reminds her to bring in all of her medicines and supplements.

When she arrives for her first visit, she finds parking easily and notices that there are plenty of accessible spaces in the lot. She enters the building through an automatic door and sees wheelchairs placed nearby for those who need them. There is a pleasing mural on the wall just inside the entranceway.

As she enters the waiting room, she observes natural light and wall hangings with relaxing images. Current magazines and up-to-date educational materials are available as well as coffee and tea. Comfortable chairs are placed in conversational arrangements.

At the first visit, the receptionist asks whether she would like help in filling out forms. Mrs. Rooney notes that the forms are simple and understandable and is able to proceed without help.

Next a medical assistant reviews all of the medicines Mrs. Rooney brought and enters relevant information into an electronic health record. Then the doctor reviews with Mrs. Rooney the medical history form she has completed and asks her what she understands about her conditions. After discussing her current symptoms, the doctor explains the treatment options, and together they create a care plan. The doctor asks Mrs. Rooney to explain in her own words how she will take her medicines and the complications she might anticipate. The doctor clarifies any confusion and then asks her again to share her understanding.

When the doctor leaves, a nurse enters the room, asks Mrs. Rooney about any remaining questions, and reviews with her a one-page handout on key points about medicines and the treatment plan.

The nurse or another health educator then gives Mrs. Rooney a copy of her medicine schedule to keep on her refrigerator and guides her through an easy-to-use personal health record. This includes her health information in plain language and simple interactive tutorials. The nurse also refers Mrs. Rooney to a diabetes education program.

Before Mrs. Rooney leaves, a scheduling assistant makes an appointment for her to return in three months. The following week, a member of the patient support team calls Mrs. Rooney to confirm the referral and appointment, to ensure that she is taking her medicines properly, and to verify that she was able to use her personal health record.

Between visits Mrs. Rooney takes her medicines regularly, undertakes the personal health record's interactive learning activities related to nutrition and physical activity, and participates in a diabetes peer support group offered by her neighborhood YWCA. When Mrs. Rooney returns for her annual wellness visit, she is confident in her ability to manage her conditions and ready to engage further with providers to improve her health.

This simple story encompasses the key components of patient engagement, summarized in the following Key Points. It also touches on the healing environment, the subject of chapter 7.

KEY POINTS

- Population health management is a key patient engagement strategy.
- SDOH can be used to identify nonmedical gaps in community services that impact health and well-being.
- Treat the whole person: mind, body, and spirit.
- Meet patients where they are through health literacy techniques.
- Understanding how diversity influences the patient's perception of their care and treatment will provide a better platform for the care process.

- Include patients in advisory councils, process improvement teams, and safety forums.
- Patients with chronic pain, mental health conditions, and chronic disease can benefit from a Whole Health approach.
- We must partner with family and friends who act as caregivers to create better health for our patients.
- Critical to engaging our patients is ensuring that they have access to the information that they need to be active partners in their healthcare.
- Use technology to open up avenues of engagement.

REFERENCES

Bokhour, B., J. Hyde, D. Mohr, and S. Zeliot. 2020. "Whole Health System of Care Evaluation—a Progress Report on Outcomes of the WHS Pilot at 18 Flagship Sites." US Department of Veterans Affairs. www.va.gov/WHOLEHEALTH/docs/EPCCWholeHealthSystemofCareEvaluation-2020-02-18FINAL_508.pdf.

Cohen, S. 2014. "The Concentration of Health Care Expenditures and Related Expenses for Costly Medical Conditions, 2012." Published October. Agency for Healthcare Research and Quality. www.ncbi.nlm.nih.gov/books/NBK470837/.

Delbanco, T. 2016. "How the 'OpenNotes' Initiative Is Changing the Way Patients and Doctors Work Together." Commonwealth Fund. Published March 18. www.commonwealthfund.org/publications/journal-article/2016/mar/how-opennotes-initiative-changing-way-patients-and-doctors.

Frampton, S. B., S. Guastello, L. Hoy, M. Naylor, S. Sheridan, and M. Johnston-Fleece. 2017. "Harnessing Evidence and Experience to Change Culture: A Guiding Framework for Patient and Family Engaged Care." *NAM Perspectives.* Published January 31. https://nam.edu/wp-content/uploads/2017/01/Harnessing-Evidence-and-Experience-to-Change-Culture-A-Guiding-Framework-for-Patient-and-Family-Engaged-Care.pdf.

Greene, J., J. Hibbard, R. Sacks, V. Overton, and C. Parrotta. 2015. "When Patient Activation Levels Change, Health Outcomes and Costs Change, Too." *Health Affairs* 34 (3): 431–7.

Office of Disease Prevention and Health Promotion. 2020. *Healthy People 2020.* www.healthypeople.gov.

World Health Organization. 2020. "Constitution of the World Health Organization." *Basic Documents, 49th Edition.* Updated May 31, 2019. https://apps.who.int/gb/bd/pdf_files/BD_49th-en.pdf#page=6.

CHAPTER 7

Designing an Evidence-Based Healing Environment

IMAGINE THIS SCENARIO: Patients check in for appointments from home or work, or some other remote location, before they leave. Arriving at the parking lot, which has piped-in music, they scan a barcode to confirm arrival. The staff is expecting them.

The waiting room is warm and welcoming, with rocking chairs and a fish tank. Soft music plays in the background. Yet no waiting is necessary, as the staff is ready and the patient is brought back to the exam room right away.

The patient reaches the room via a dedicated corridor, which forms a perimeter around the staff activities in the center of the office. All needed services are brought to the patient in that single room except when an X-ray is required. A dermatology consult is arranged using telehealth. Then, at the end of the provider visit, the patient circles back through the corridor to the reception desk, where they are efficiently checked out. Or, even better, they can check out and receive discharge instructions and educational materials from a printer right in the exam room.

How close to today's reality is this scenario? The primary care practice setting is evolving to incorporate more efficient healing designs. Much evidence in the literature supports the innovations now being used to design the built environment so that it optimizes healing.

> The primary care practice setting is evolving to incorporate more efficient healing designs.

In this chapter we will share well-considered elements that make for a nurturing and healing environment, along with our experience with onstage–offstage design.

PRINCIPLES OF HEALING DESIGN

Roslyn Lindheim, a professor of architecture at the University of California, espoused a set of principles for the design of healthcare settings (Arneill and Frasca-Beaulieu 2003):

- Welcome the patient's family and friends.
- Value human beings over technology.
- Enable patients to fully participate as partners in their care.
- Provide flexibility to personalize each patient's care.
- Encourage caregivers to be responsive to patients.
- Foster a connection to nature and beauty.

These objectives become the foundation of patient-centered care facility design. Let's expand on them to consider all elements of the patient and staff experience.

Design Objectives Focused on the Patient Experience

Centering the patient in the primary care experience requires a shift in the design approach toward the following objectives:

- Create a calm, healing environment.
- Reduce waiting and wasteful or redundant activities.
- Value the patient's time by facilitating processes that allow them to be seen when convenient for them, increasing provider–patient face time, and right-sizing the patient care areas.
- Include the patient's accompanying family member or caregiver when rooming them.
- Create a patient "one-stop approach."
- Tailor care delivery to patient needs with a balanced approach: telephone/virtual care, shared medical appointments, e-consultation, and face-to-face care.

Design Objectives for Team-Based Care

The patient-centered medical home (PCMH) team is at the heart of this primary care model. How do we design the space to provide maximum support to the team? Consider these objectives from the Veterans Health Administration (VHA 2015):

- Collocate staff to promote collegiality, communication, and consultation.

- Create team-based office work space with a logical and efficient flow between exam rooms and team work settings that affords direct visual connection among staff.
- Provide a range of work spaces to accommodate multiple needs: team-based work, huddles, and solo activities.

Design Objectives for Access and Healing

Healthcare delivery approaches and patient needs are always evolving. In addition to designing a facility and care processes that enhance patient-centered and team-based care, we aligned with specific design objectives to improve access to care. Objectives created to ensure that the space can adapt to changing requirements, while promoting access and efficiency, include the following:

- Standardizing room designs. Universal exam and procedure rooms include the functionality and capacity to support virtual/telehealth delivery.
- Providing space for shared medical appointments. Waiting rooms include an extra room that can be converted to value-added space with virtual/telehealth capability for patient education and group care. These shared medical appointments, conducted for cohorts of patients with chronic diseases (e.g., hypertension, diabetes), are effective in managing population health initiatives.
- Supporting a modular approach to overall clinic design and space planning.
- Designing all spaces to be adaptable to future needs with minimal construction.

Additional features of the clinic include ceiling-mounted computers that facilitate face-to-face interactions between the provider and the patient better than traditional wheeled computer workstations can. Providers are able to swing these devices from the exam table to the patient seating area in the exam rooms, making eye contact as they enter their notes. Alternatively, if the providers use laptops, a table on wheels can give the same flexibility. The screen should be visible to the patient for educational purposes.

These design elements highlight the essential connection between function and form, optimizing the space to enable the primary care team to provide outstanding clinical care. In addition, the model permits adaptation to varying needs from clinic to clinic. Some of these primary care clinics provide physical and occupational therapy services, others optometry and audiology.

Codesign

Whether you are planning a new facility or renovating the current one, a good place to start is with the concept of codesign: inviting patients, families, and staff to participate in designing or renovating the clinical space. Among the different approaches one can take is to invite patients and staff to be a part of the design team from the start. Another is to conduct focus groups to get input, then invite all parties to experience prototypes and mock-ups, then modify the design using their feedback. You can also employ a combination of these approaches. The key is to use an iterative, interactive, and inclusive approach—the three I's.

> The key is to use an iterative, interactive, and inclusive approach—the three I's.

Efficiency

Designs that achieve the preceding objectives promote efficiency, thus saving staff and patients time. Services come to the patient's exam room, to avoid shuffling them from room to room. I (Mary-Ellen) have observed that the average nurse's walking distance per shift drops significantly when the work area is designed to promote efficiency.

I have also conducted Lean Kaizen events during which I have asked physicians to observe a nurse for an hour and draw a picture of what they see. Inevitably that picture is a spaghetti diagram illustrating the additional steps a nurse needs to cover because equipment, supplies, and the tools needed for their job are not at their fingertips.

Access to Nature

A healing environment admits natural light while providing access to nature. This could include an atrium feature, skylights, plenty of windows (glazed to filter natural light), and plants. Views of nature can help reduce stress by producing a sense of calm. Soft colors are found to promote quiet.

> Views of nature can help reduce stress by producing a sense of calm. Soft colors are found to promote quiet.

And don't forget about the outside of the facility. Nicely landscaped grounds with plantings at the entrance provide a warm, calming welcome. Rooftop gardens, walking paths, and labyrinths can provide a contemplative space for patients, friends, and family members as well as staff.

As we continue to make facilities smoke free, we need to monitor our entrances for smoking debris several times a day. Cigarette butts send the wrong message when we are trying to promote healthy lifestyles.

Clutter

Physical and visual clutter can make our patients more anxious. Are the clinic hallways and exam rooms neat and tidy? Or are they used to store equipment and supplies?

All too often I see memos, notices, and information bulletins plastered over the walls throughout the clinic. Many are not current. This volume distracts from the information that is critical for our staff and patients. Post notices judiciously and attractively in a central location so staff and patients know where to find information.

Way-Finding

How do we open access to our facilities and make it easy for patients to navigate them? Way-finding, or the ways in which people orient themselves in physical space and navigate from place to place, starts with exterior signage that is clear and easy to understand. Ensure parking is close by and plentiful. Make your entrance accessible with a covered patient drop-off. Even better, offer valet parking.

A motion-sensing automatic door with wheelchairs placed conveniently nearby helps patients who have difficulty ambulating on their own. Nothing is more frustrating than trying to find your way around in a new setting with little or confusing signage.

Speaking of signs, I have seen large STOP signs in some clinics right in front of the check-in area. Our patients often arrive anxious and vulnerable, unsure of what is going to happen to them during their visit, what bad news they might get, or how their treatments might impact their lives. We don't need to do anything to increase that anxiety. Instead, a friendly sign, reading "Please wait here for the next available receptionist," is so much better than a threatening STOP sign. Directional signage should be stated in the positive.

Just as frustrating is a proliferation of directional signage that is difficult to follow. In this context, less is more. Simple, easy-to-follow signs quickly orient the patient to their new surroundings.

Some facilities use kiosks in entrance areas that provide maps to the location that the patient or visitor selects. For instance, if I want to go to the primary care clinic, I select it from the list of options and a map will print out. Other organizations have roving greeters to help patients find their way.

Color coding also can be used effectively. My orthopedic physician is a partner in a very busy practice. His area is color-coded yellow, so I just follow the directional signs to the yellow area.

The latest innovation in way-finding includes GPS technology, apps that allow users to search for points of interest and get the best route to their destination, saving time for patients and staff alike.

Quiet and Privacy

Busy clinics will want to promote both quiet and privacy through design and practice. Past designs often included a barrier between the patient and the staff member at the check-in desk. These have long been a pet peeve of mine because they send messages such as "I am afraid of you," "I don't have time for you," or "You are not welcome here."

These barriers are designed with staff in mind, not patients. There are other ways to make staff feel safe, if that's an issue in a particular clinic setting, such as those in high-crime areas. Here are a few options:

- Training and skill-building in managing disruptive patients, conflict resolution, and customer service
- Panic alarms
- Designating and drilling escape routes

In this friendlier, more welcoming model, partitions still exist between workstations in the check-in area to ensure auditory privacy. Another healing-design feature is to offer patient kiosks in the waiting room for quick and easy check-in.

Healing Arts

Numerous healing arts and positive distractions can enhance the patient experience. Again, natural light, plants, and water features all make for a more welcoming space.

Tasteful art (paintings, photographs, sculpture) can be relaxing, but a word of caution: There is a science to this. Images of nature and smiling or sympathetic human faces work much better than abstract images or urban scenes, which can produce stress. Most people want to see images that make them feel happy or calm.

The first time I walked into one of the VHA's new PCMH clinics, I was a bit startled by the images of military service, as they don't exactly fit the "healing design" formula of nature themes. However, I quickly learned that these images provided a connection for the veterans seeking care. They felt at home, understood. This illustrates the importance of including your patients in the design process. One size does not fit all.

Music can be soothing in the right setting, allowing the patient to unwind and release tension. I have also seen the use of exam room ceiling tiles with relaxing images of nature. In fact, my dental office has them, and a colleague uses them to focus patients on something pleasant during uncomfortable procedures, such as Pap smears.

As for your waiting rooms, ensure they have plenty of current reading and educational materials. Nothing says "we don't care" like magazines that are two years old. Coffee, tea, water, and vending machines with healthy choices are always welcome, as are free Wi-Fi and charging stations.

I often see a play area with books and toys available to occupy small children. And, yes, even pet therapy has a place in the primary care setting. Therapy dog visits in an outpatient setting can greatly reduce pain and emotional distress for chronic pain patients. Such dog visits can also significantly improve emotional upset and feelings of well-being in family and friends accompanying patients to appointments. And let's not forget clinic staff—they, too, can benefit from pet visits.

In sum, clinic spaces should make patients and their families feel as welcome and supported as possible so that the environment enhances the experience, rather than detracting from it. A healing environment enables all involved in patient care to provide for the whole patient: body, mind and spirit.

> A healing environment enables all involved in patient care to provide for the whole patient: body, mind and spirit.

ONSTAGE–OFFSTAGE

Increasingly, healthcare facilities are looking to organizations outside their field for best practices that can be used to improve various aspects of patient care, such as throughput and safety. One such best practice is the Onstage–Offstage design developed by the VHA (2015).

Taken from the Disney model, this design is meant to enhance the patient experience, improving the flow of services to the patient. If you have ever visited Disneyland or Disney World, you probably know that many of the support functions and behind-the-scenes activities take place "offstage." We never see them. What we see is the "show," onstage.

That's the concept here. It's meant to be welcoming and efficient while maximizing the face time between the patient and the care team. The patient pathway, or the "onstage" area, is situated around the outer hallways of the clinic and consists of the registration/check-in desk, waiting area, exam rooms, and a space for shared medical appointments. Patient hallways provide easy and separate access to exam rooms.

Even though the patient pathway is situated around the periphery of the building, the design puts patients at the center of care by bringing all services—including labs and ECG testing—directly to them in their exam room. This one-stop-shop approach allows providers to tailor the delivery of primary care and specialized services to the individual and is far more comprehensive and convenient for patients.

In this design, exam rooms are built to accommodate scooters and larger wheelchairs. They are also large enough for patients to bring their family or a caregiver to an appointment. The idea is to improve flow such that there aren't long waits in the waiting room or the exam rooms.

Staff Spaces for Work and Rest

Comfortable staff work areas that situate team members for the best opportunity to interact and collaborate are integral to this design. Locating PCMH teams in centralized pods affords increased communication and collaboration while improving efficiency and protecting the privacy of patient health information. Private offices are located adjacent to the pod to provide a quiet space when needed.

The clinic setup creates a collegial space for teams to consult one another about their patients' care, prepare warm handoffs, and make decisions in real time, all of which improve patient flow and other efficiencies.

Staff can also be supported by using the most up-to-date technology in quiet and engaging workspaces. For instance, huddle spaces with whiteboards are great locations for teams to kick-off the work day. Commonly used supplies are stored near the "offstage" area, with access controlled through security and privacy improvements.

> After all, if we don't take care of our staff, they can't take care of our patients.

Let's consider briefly what it means to create a healing environment for staff by focusing on the break room. The evidence tells us that workers and the work benefit from brief rests and power naps. So provide a quiet, restful place for staff that doesn't double as the locker room, the lunch room, and the training space. This shows that you truly care about staff's well-being. After all, if we don't take care of our staff, they can't take care of our patients.

Let's Take a Walk

To illustrate and summarize the features of this design, let's take a virtual walk through the on-stage, off-stage design model.

- **First entry:** First impressions are positive as the patient encounters intuitive way-finding and a calm, quiet, nurturing environment.
- **Reception, greeting, and check-in:** Staff greet the patient warmly and with a smile in a pleasing setting that promotes efficiency and privacy.
- **Patient transition area:** Waiting is minimized before the patient is roomed, along with a possible family member or caregiver. Appropriate patient education is seamlessly integrated into the care episode.
- **Corridors and connections:** The separation of patient and staff corridors enhances privacy and quiet. Patient corridors are sized to accommodate wheelchairs and other assistive devices.
- **Separation of flow:** Patient movement patterns are visually and physically separated from staff and offstage circulation. The use of noise mitigation materials and strategies reduces noise and stress.
- **Appointment, follow-up planning, and checkout:** The patient care room is the hub for these activities with all supplies and equipment needed at hand. Printers are available to provide discharge instructions and educational materials. The patient is escorted out by staff to ensure they know where to go. This provides one last opportunity for patients to ask questions.

Patient and Care Team Feedback

As described by Bondura and Piche (2019), this onstage–offstage framework emphasizes provision of care that is accessible, timely, coordinated, continuous, comprehensive, and compassionate. Our clinic facilities and care teams make primary care and the PCMH the foundation of healthcare delivery, with the patient at the center of the primary care team. This framework has become our starting design standard for creating functional, efficient, nurturing, and pleasing environments, and it will

> Our clinic facilities and care teams make primary care and the PCMH the foundation of healthcare delivery, with the patient at the center of the primary care team.

continue to evolve through ongoing collaboration and user/customer feedback. Improvements in our newest clinic include integrated white noise throughout and higher partitions in the team work area for enhanced auditory privacy. This design approach engages patients on many levels.

As patients settled into this new look, many contributed mementos and personal art that have helped to make these clinics their own. Patients routinely give feedback on surveys stating, "Wonderful place, wonderful care, wonderful people!" and "Very impressive, beautiful clinic! Great care!" Patients aren't the only people pleased with this innovative clinic. The staff also has welcomed this highly functional work environment. They see the design of the clinic as a big improvement in patient and staff privacy and safety. (See a sample schematic in appendix I.)

WHAT'S NEXT?

Let's expand our view beyond the single clinic to the PCMH "neighborhood." My health insurer recently opened a new medical facility not far from my home that they are calling a "one-stop doctor's office experience for patients." Along with primary and specialty services, this neighborhood includes amenities such as a pharmacy, education center, lab, nook for kids, telemedicine pods, and a community room where local organizations can gather. It is located in an easily accessible area central to the three major cities in the area.

The pharmacy offers onsite prescription pickup and consultations, free home delivery, and over-the-counter medications. The tele-pods are soundproof, insulated booths where patients can sit and speak with a specialist regarding services not often provided in the primary care setting such as behavioral health.

Consultation rooms are staffed with health insurance reps to address benefit questions and assist with claims, or to sign patients up for Medicare or Medicaid. The education center is equipped with computers and preapproved, provider-recommended websites so that patients can research diagnosis-related information.

It doesn't stop there! Cozy fireplaces, valet parking, car charging stations, and a refreshment center all add to the healing environment.

LET'S GO SHOPPING!

To wrap up chapters 4 through 7, let's ask ourselves, "How do we know that our efforts in engaging staff/provider/patient/family and creating a healing environment are effective?" Typically, surveys and focus groups are used to generate qualitative and quantitative feedback on what matters most to our stakeholders. Complaints are another good source of issues that are pain points for our patients.

Why not take the next step and engage in mystery shopping? Fresh eyes can provide a clear perspective on what is working and what needs to be improved. You can enlist an intern, members of your patient/family advisory council, community representatives, or a consultant.

Here's how it works:

- The shopper is "undercover" as a relative or friend, accompanying a patient who has a clinic appointment.
- The shopper has a list of criteria to check during the encounter.
- Criteria include environmental elements starting with way-finding, parking, access, comfort, quiet, and privacy.
- Aspects of staff engagement include communication, timeliness, giving the patient options and choice, and honoring their preferences.
- All components of the visit are observed and evaluated: registration, waiting room experience, rooming, provider encounter, and discharge.
- The shopper takes pictures of the environment (avoiding the exposure of private health information and actual patients in the clinic), noting strong practices (access to nature, comfortable seating, good signage) and weak areas (dirty bathrooms, stained ceiling tiles, cluttered hallways).

Through these detailed observations, the shopper can provide an enlightening look into your clinic. Use this information to build on strong practices, improve those that aren't hitting the mark, and recognize those staff who demonstrate good alignment with your customer service standards. (See appendix J for a sample "shopping list.")

KEY POINTS

- Include patients, families, and staff in an iterative, interactive, and inclusive design approach.
- Onstage–offstage design enhances the patient and staff experience, improving the flow of services.
- Healing design strategies include access to nature, positive distractions, improved way-finding, and reducing clutter and noise.
- A healing environment enables all involved in patient care to provide for the whole patient: body, mind, and spirit.
- Mystery shopping can be a useful adjunct to surveys and focus groups.

REFERENCES

Arneill, B., and K. Frasca-Beaulieu. 2003. In *Designing and Practicing Patient-Centered Care*, edited by S. Frampton, L. Gilpin, and P. Charmell, 163–92. San Francisco: Jossey-Bass.

Bondura, K., and M. E. Piche. 2019. "Facility, Care Team Design Promotes Healing." *Healthcare Executive*. Published July/August. https://healthcareexecutive.org.

US Department of Veterans Affairs. 2015. "PACT Space Module Design Guide." Published June. www.cfm.va.gov/til/dGuide/dgPACT.pdf.

CHAPTER 8

Key Performance Indicators

Key performance indicators (KPIs), also known as metrics or performance measures, are used to evaluate the performance of a healthcare organization. KPIs can help the organization achieve its mission and goals while ensuring high-quality outcomes as healthcare shifts toward value-based care. This chapter will provide a comprehensive overview of KPIs in the increasingly competitive healthcare environment.

WHAT ARE KPIs?

KPIs tell the organization, insurance companies, and patients how well it is fulfilling its mission and meeting benchmarks. They provide concrete evidence of the quality of care the organization is providing. KPIs yield data to gauge various components of healthcare and, when successfully executed, give the organization an opportunity to achieve a competitive advantage in its market.

KPI development is commonly guided by these three factors:

- Metrics specific to the organization
- State or federal regulations
- Contractual agreements

WHY ARE KPIs ESSENTIAL?

The healthcare industry has become increasingly value oriented. When shopping for healthcare, today's savvy patients want to know what an organization offers and how it performs. KPIs document and validate the organization's performance on different measures, assuring patients the organization will meet their care expectations.

In addition to offering a grading system, KPIs enable patients to partner with an organization whose goals align with their own. For example, a millennial seeking immediate access to healthcare might be more attracted to the technological capabilities of an organization, because they want healthcare at their fingertips. By contrast, an older patient with a poorly controlled chronic disease may be more interested in the outcomes an organization has achieved in managing this disease.

For the organization, KPIs create the opportunity to provide patients with evidence and validation of its success, providing it a chance to show how it measures against other organizations. They also demonstrate the operation's investment in performance improvement and good outcomes. Last, KPIs give the organization a way to track and improve services.

UNDERSTANDING KPIs

Before selecting KPIs, the organization should research well-established and widely used healthcare metrics. These can be found through the Centers for Medicare & Medicaid Services (CMS) and the National Committee for Quality Assurance (NCQA). It is beneficial to select from existing metrics as these are proven to be reliable and valid.

Using CMS Measures

CMS's Core Quality Measures Collaborative has identified a fundamental set of key performance measures, termed Core Measures. The purpose of these measures is to aid improvement efforts in value-based payment programs. Core Measures are categorized as follows:

- Cardiovascular Care
- Diabetes
- Care Coordination/Patient Safety
- Prevention and Wellness
- Utilization and Cost/Overuse
- Patient Experience
- Behavioral Health
- Pulmonary
- Readmissions

Exhibit 8.1: Centers for Medicare & Medicaid Services Metrics as Quality Measures

Cardiovascular Care
- Statin use
- Controlling high blood pressure

Diabetes
- HbA1c poor control (>9.0%)
- Eye exam
- HbA1c testing
- Medical attention for nephropathy

Care Coordination/Patient Safety
- Medication reconciliation

Prevention and Wellness
- Cervical cancer screening
- Breast cancer screening
- Colorectal cancer screening
- One-time screening for hepatitis C virus
- Tobacco use screening

Utilization and Cost/Overuse
- Use of imaging studies for low back pain

Patient Experience
- CAHPS clinician and group surveys

Behavioral Health
- Depression screening
- Alcohol use screening

Pulmonary
- Avoidance of antibiotic with acute bronchitis

Readmissions
- Plan all-cause readmissions

Note: CAHPS = Consumer Assessment of Healthcare Providers and Systems.
Source: Data from Centers for Medicare & Medicaid Services (2020).

These categories are further divided into specific metrics. Exhibit 8.1 shows some of the metrics CMS has defined as quality measures.

These are well-established metrics that overlap with those endorsed by NCQA. This list is not exhaustive but does adequately represent metrics that are meaningful to patients and providers. It also captures a large volume of patients with commonly seen issues.

Using HEDIS Measures

NCQA has developed one of the most widely used tools for performance improvement: the HEDIS (Healthcare Effectiveness Data and Information Set). HEDIS offers 90 measures divided into the following key domains of care:

- Effectiveness of Care
- Access/Availability of Care
- Utilization and Risk-Adjusted Utilization
- Health Plan Descriptive Information
- Measures Reporting Using Electronic Clinical Data Systems

As with the Core Measures, these six domains drill down further to more specific metrics. Exhibit 8.2 lists examples of commonly used HEDIS metrics in the primary care setting.

Exhibit 8.2: Commonly Used HEDIS Metrics

Effectiveness of Care	**Prevention and screening**
	- Adult BMI
	- Breast cancer screening
	- Cervical cancer screening
	- Colorectal cancer screening
	- Childhood immunization status
	Respiratory conditions
	- Pharmacotherapy management of COPD exacerbation
	- Medication management for people with asthma
	Cardiovascular conditions
	- Controlling high blood pressure
	- Statin therapy
	Diabetes
	- Comprehensive diabetes care
	Musculoskeletal conditions
	- Osteoporosis testing and management in older women
	Behavioral health
	- Antidepressant medication management
	- Follow-up after hospitalization for mental illness
	- Adherence to antipsychotic medications
	Medication management and care coordination
	- Medication reconciliation postdischarge
	- Annual monitoring for patients on persistent medications

(continued)

Exhibit 8.2: Commonly Used HEDIS Metrics (*continued*)

	Overuse/appropriateness
	• Non-recommended PSA-based screening in older men
	• Use of imaging studies for low back pain
	• Use of opioids at high dosages
	• Avoidance of antibiotic in adults with acute bronchitis
	Measures collected through Medicare health outcome surveys
	• Fall risk management
	• Management of urinary incontinence in older adults
	Measures collected through CAHPS health plan survey
	• Flu vaccinations
	• Medical assistance with smoking and tobacco cessation
Access/Availability of Care	• Adults' access to preventive/ambulatory health services
	• Annual dental visit
	• Prenatal and postpartum care
	• Initiation and engagement of alcohol and other drug abuse or dependence treatment
Utilization	• Child and adolescent well-care visits
	• Mental health utilization
	• Antibiotic utilization
Risk-Adjusted Utilization	• Plan all-cause readmissions
	• Acute hospital utilization
	• Emergency department utilization
	• Hospitalization for potentially preventable complications
Measures Reported Using Electronic Clinical Data Systems	• Utilization of PHQ-9 to monitor depression symptoms
	• Unhealthy alcohol use screening and follow-up
	• Adult immunization status

Note: BMI = body mass index; CAHPS = Consumer Assessment of Healthcare Providers and Systems; COPD = chronic obstructive pulmonary disease; HEDIS = Healthcare Effectiveness Data and Information Set; PHQ-9 = Patient Health Questionnaire–9; PSA = prostate-specific antigen.
Source: Data from National Committee for Quality Assurance (2021).

These categories can be broken down in more detail. For instance, the comprehensive diabetes care category under Effectiveness of Care assesses adults aged 18 to 75 years with diabetes (type 1 or 2) who had one or more of the following:

1. HbA1c testing
2. HbA1c poor control (>9.0%)
3. HbA1c control (<8.0%)
4. HbA1c control (<7.0%) for a selected population
5. Eye exam (retinal) performed

6. Medical attention for nephropathy
7. BP control (<140/90 mmHg)

Practical Application and Additional Benefits of HEDIS Measures

Any organization can easily adopt these specific diabetes measures, which is useful because diabetes affects a significant amount of the patient population. By selecting these measures, the organization can have a great impact on a high volume of patients. Another benefit of selecting these measures is that data are easy to obtain. Through provider scorecards (see chapter 5 for more details), the organization can easily bring awareness to these metrics. Using a strong health information system, primary care teams should easily be able to access these metrics and determine the outlier patients that cause them to "fail" the metric. Such patients should be targeted in an effort to optimize their diabetes control and reduce diabetes complications, both of which lead to better performance outcomes.

HEDIS also provides data through the State of Healthcare Quality Report for each domain category (commercial HMO, commercial PPO, Medicaid HMO, Medicare HMO, PPO). This helps the organization know the standards of every health plan for each calendar year, information that can aid in determining a realistic goal for each metric.

WHAT IS NEEDED TO ADOPT KPIs?

Renowned management thinker Peter Drucker said, "You can't manage what you can't measure." This speaks to the need for a strong health information system.

Once the organization has chosen its KPIs, it must develop a data monitoring and collection system specific to the KPIs. For example, if communication is chosen as the desired KPI, there must be a way to measure and collect relevant communication data. Measurement tools include databases, surveys, interviews, audits, and rating scales.

It is key that the measurement tools selected have proven reliability and validity. To ensure reliability, the tool must yield the same result each time. To be valid, it must measure what it is intended to measure. The tools also must accurately reflect what is being measured.

Last, the organization must consider variability. Variability looks at the range of data, from the highest to the lowest values. For example, data for antibiotic prescription rates may range from 0 to 100 percent. The denominator or total number of patients each provider sees likely varies. Data showing a prescriber with 100 percent antibiotic prescribing rates may be alarming at first glance, but when the data are reviewed more closely, you may find that the prescriber only saw one patient. This tiny sample size skews the data and does not truly reflect overall antibiotic-prescribing rates.

Standard deviations are used to determine variability of data. The closer the data values are to the average value, the less variability there is in the data. The antibiotics example depicts the standard deviation from the mean—in this case, the average prescriber rate for antibiotics.

To make sure all these statistical components are accurately and reliably collected, the organization must have a robust information system.

Invest in Strong Information Systems

The use of electronic medical records has become vital for sharing data to improve patient outcomes. However, the data are only useful when they can be captured and turned into useful information. Therefore, the information system used should be sophisticated and reliable. The information systems available for use can be categorized as follows:

- Administrative
- Clinical
- Human resources
- Financial
- Patient experience
- Imaging
- Decision support

When choosing an information system, ensure that the system measures what is needed for the organization's selected KPIs.

Exhibit 8.3 provides a helpful checklist to evaluate systems and determine which is best for the organization.

Ultimately, the information system chosen by the organization must support its goals and mission.

> Ultimately, the information system chosen by the organization must support its goals and mission.

Data Triggers Are Critical

Data triggers greatly improve the performance of an organization and are critical for patient safety. They signal the organization when further analysis is needed, such as a root-cause analysis or additional chart reviews. The ability to measure the level of actual or potential harm the organization has caused is a must. Therefore,

Exhibit 8.3: Information System Checklist

Interface	Does the system interface with the organization's current system?
Accreditation and regulatory compliance	Does the system support accreditation and regulatory compliance? Is it able to pull data for quality, safety, and performance improvement? Does it support the needs of credentialing?
Multi-user access	Does the system allow for multiple users to have access to the same programs at the same time?
Triggers	Does the system allow for the development of "triggers" to determine when data fall above or below threshold? Does it allow for critical alerts?
Algorithms	Does the system allow for algorithm-based processing?
Networking	Does the system allow for networking capabilities with other organizations?
Cost-effectiveness	Is the system cost-effective for the organization?
Current and retrospective data	Does the system allow the organization to look at and compare current data with old data?

it is imperative that the organization invest in a health information system able to capture triggers and identify the following events:

- **Adverse event:** Unintended or unfavorable occurrence that can be life threatening or require a patient to become hospitalized. Has the ability to worsen a patient's health or condition or to cause congenital disorders, disability, or a prolonged hospital stay. Commonly seen examples in the primary care setting are adverse medication events.
- **Sentinel event:** An unexpected death, or a major health impairment expected to be chronic or to affect the patient's quality of life indefinitely.

In addition to reporting through health information systems, triggers can also be reported via feedback from patients and staff. Tracking triggers over time allows the organization to know if process improvements are increasing patient safety.

Benchmarking

Once the appropriate information system has been chosen for data collection, the next step is data analysis. An important element for analysis is benchmarking. Through external benchmarking, the organization can compare performance with that of its competitors to verify it is performing optimally. This also gives patients and insurance companies a sense of where the organization stands among its competition in various fields.

Internal benchmarking is commonly done among providers and can be accomplished in several ways. Many organizations compare providers in the same specialty while consulting national rates from other providers who work in a similar primary care setting. (See chapter 5 for an example of how to use provider scorecards for benchmarking.)

> Through external benchmarking, the organization can compare performance with that of its competitors to verify it is performing optimally.

Through benchmarking, the organization can also identify trends and create goals while continuously measuring progress. A constant comparison must be made against best-performing organizations in order to drive success.

Other Forms of Data Measurement and Collection

A health information system, although important, is not the only source of data measurement. Other methods include the following:

- Administrative data can be useful in the primary care setting when looking at billing and workload credit.
- Medical record audits can be a valuable tool in collecting different types of data, specifically data that are difficult to capture in a health information system. Although more time intensive than other methods, audits provide a good snapshot of the data.
- Reports from external resources such as accreditation bodies, governing bodies such as the Centers for Disease Control and Prevention, and state or national best-practice organizations can also provide quality data.
- Patient surveys can provide valuable information and perspectives on quality of care. The Consumer Assessment of Healthcare Providers and Systems (CAHPS) surveys provide qualitative data related to the patient's experience. Direct feedback from patients and families is invaluable information that provides the organization with insight into its strengths and weaknesses from consumers' point of view.

The Significance of CAHPS

The Agency for Healthcare Research and Quality (2020) provides several patient experience surveys known as CAHPS. Conducting such surveys lets the organization know if it is meeting patients' expectations and needs. Patient experience is an important quality indicator because patient satisfaction influences not only clinical outcomes but also patient retention and medical malpractice claims. The following are the measures from the CAHPS ambulatory care surveys:

- CAHPS Health Plan Survey Measures
- CAHPS Clinician and Group Survey Measures
- CAHPS Cancer Care Survey Measures
- CAHPS Surgical Care Survey Measures
- CAHPS Dental Plan Survey Measures
- Experience of Care and Health Outcomes Survey Measures
- CAHPS American Indian Survey Measures

CAHPS and the Patient-Centered Medical Home

Each of the CAHPS surveys ask important questions, but the CAHPS Clinician and Group Survey Measures focuses specifically on access, provider communication, and coordination of care. This aligns with the patient-centered medical home (PCMH) model. (See chapters 2 and 3 for more information on the PCMH.) This CAHPS survey can make the organization aware of how well it is implementing the PCMH and help determine if improvements need to be made.

INTERPRETING DATA FOR DECISION MAKING

KPIs provide a wealth of information on outcomes and processes. To optimize decision making, the organization must be able to interpret the data and assess how they relate to its current processes. The aim is to turn meaningful data into useful information to help guide the decision-making process.

Structure, Process, and Outcomes

Once the organization creates useful information from the data, it can use the information for performance monitoring and improvement. The Donabedian model (see chapter 3) has greatly contributed to improvements in healthcare quality and safety through the use of performance measures. According to Donabedian, healthcare can be assessed and improved through a three-part model:

1. **Structure:** The physical and organizational resources the organization uses to deliver healthcare. This includes everything from the staff and equipment to available financial resources.

2. **Process:** How care is delivered to the patient, including services provided to the patient and how well they are carried out. The focus in this category is typically compliance with guidelines and evidence-based practice.
3. **Outcomes:** The status of patient and population health resulting from interactions and interventions by the healthcare organization, including the overall impact the organization has and whether it is positive or negative (Berwick and Fox 2016).

The Donabedian model is further enhanced by using KPIs that capture data and trends for various factors in these three parts. To successfully navigate this model and start to make changes and improvements, however, the organization must get buy-in from staff.

ENCOURAGING STAFF INVOLVEMENT WITH METRICS

Much like a SMART goal (see chapter 3 for more information), metrics for KPIs should be realistic, attainable, and timely, but also meaningful to staff and patients. To set meaningful goals, the organization should ask the staff to be involved in selecting metrics that are impactful to them. Do not forget: Staff are stakeholders as well. This ensures they are invested in improving the metrics and that the organization picks the correct metric. The staff, whether it be a group of nurses, providers, social workers, or another constituency, can develop their own plan to achieve these goals, thereby winning buy-in from other team members, which in turn leads to better results.

Exhibit 8.4 lists some of the typical metrics the organization can anticipate from registered nurse stakeholders. These are adapted from CMS.

Exhibit 8.4: Metrics Applicable to Registered Nurses

Goal	Target Population
Improving the rate of HbA1c annual lab values in patients with diabetes.	High rate of patients with diabetes who do not have their annual diabetes labs drawn.
Increasing the rate of annual dental visits.	High rates of poor dentition in patients with poor access to a dentist.
Decreasing high doses of opioids.	High rates of opioid overdose.
Increasing blood pressure control in heart disease patients.	Heart disease patients with blood pressure readings of >140/90 mmHg in the last year.
Medical reconciliation at each visit.	Patients at risk for medication confusion and errors.

Quality Measures for the Organization

The organization should drive company-wide goals with high-impact, high-volume outcomes. For example, hypertension is the number-one diagnosis in the primary care setting and can potentially damage patients' health if not properly controlled. This metric affects every provider, along with a high volume of patients, which is why both HEDIS and CMS focus on this metric.

Exhibit 8.5 depicts a goal and process for achieving high rates of blood pressure control.

With this type of process in place, the organization creates provider awareness of the importance of this metric, offers education and coaching to help improve prescribing practices, and involves nurses in monitoring patient blood pressure, all of which improve rates of blood pressure control.

Example Safety Initiative: Measures for Opioid Use

A hot topic right now for patient safety is opioid use. Opioids are highly addictive controlled substances that, if misused, can lead to overdose and death. The US Veterans Health Administration (VHA 2020) is tackling this issue head-on by developing an Opioid Safety Initiative that many organizations can easily model. The initiative features a portal for safe prescriber practices, patient education, and other resources that can even be accessed by patients in the privacy of their own home. The VHA also provides easily accessible data to help target patients prescribed opioids who are at risk of dependency. Exhibit 8.6 details a process for lowering the rate of opioid prescriptions as suggested by CMS.

Exhibit 8.5: Process for Improving Blood Pressure Control

Metric: Blood pressure control defined as < 140/90 mmHg
Goal: Achieve control in 80% of patients with high blood pressure

- Obtain fallout patient list.
- Educate providers on guidelines for blood pressure treatment.
- Establish a protocol to monitor fallout patients every two weeks.
- Establish mentors for providers who need assistance.
- Measure monthly to track progress.
- Update all staff monthly on progress.

Exhibit 8.6: Process for Reducing Rates of Opioid Prescribing

Metric: Reducing rates of opioid prescribing
Goal: Aim to decrease the amount of opioid prescribing by 25%

- Establish patient safety team.
- Obtain list of high-risk patients on opioids.
- Educate patients on signs of overdose and risk of taking opioids.
- Coach providers on how to handle difficult conversations with patients.
- Train providers to offer various other treatments for pain.
- Develop policy for treatment plans for patients with chronic pain.

How to Get the Ball Rolling

To effectively get buy-in and implement efforts aimed at KPIs, organizations must first create awareness. Although leadership can easily see the benefits of KPIs, they must communicate this to staff. Avoid the pitfall of moving directly to the implementation phase. Some staff will comply with changes, but others will not. Staff need to be educated on what KPIs are before they can see the value in them. Otherwise, staff will view KPIs as an additional administrative duty.

Educational in-services should be provided, and staff given the opportunity to join committees depending on the KPIs they deem meaningful to them. This creates buy-in for performance improvement activities which generates better patient outcomes.

Give Staff Tools to Improve Clinical KPIs

Let us take a closer look at blood pressure metrics, because both HEDIS and CMS focus heavily on these and most primary care organizations are likely to adopt them. It is not enough simply to push the KPI out to the staff and expect better results—as noted, awareness is the first step. Next, providers and nurses should be given the tools to help improve their patient's blood pressure scores. Through provider meetings (see chapter 5 for guidance on how to successfully start these), education on guidelines, coaching, and process implementation, staff will start to feel empowered to make needed changes to improve these scores. Last, the staff must have access to a database that allows them to determine which outlier patients to target.

Give Staff a Voice

Staff are the largest influencers and implementers of change needed for successful KPI implementation. When staff have a voice in making changes that are meaningful to them and their patients, outcomes are more achievable and more swiftly attained. Staff should have a say in how they plan to carry out changes as they are usually the ones tasked with implementing them. Staff should also have input on performance measure goals, because they know what is realistic. Nurses, for instance, can profoundly influence KPIs specific to patient experience, clinical measures, and patient safety. They are also uniquely qualified to assess the quality of care patients are receiving, because they interact with patients more than anyone else on the primary care team. Nurses therefore must have a voice in successfully implementing KPIs.

CONTINUAL IMPROVEMENTS

Measuring quality and safety is a necessity in healthcare. Each organization must prioritize these practices to provide the best patient care possible. Through a robust quality and safety program, the organization can continually improve the care that is delivered to patients and ensure good outcomes. When outcomes are measured and improved, the patient experience is enhanced. This is the ultimate form of value-based care.

Now that we have discussed KPIs and their importance, with several examples of how to successfully implement them, let us move to chapter 9 to determine which KPIs are best for your organization.

KEY POINTS

- KPIs are essential in value-based care.
- There are numerous well-established KPIs, such as those promoted by CMS and HEDIS.
- A strong health information system is needed to obtain data and create meaningful information.
- The Donabedian model provides the framework for assessing quality healthcare.
- Encouraging staff involvement yields better outcomes on performance measures.

REFERENCES

Agency for Healthcare Research and Quality. 2020. "CAHPS Measures of Patient Experience." Reviewed September. www.ahrq.gov/cahps/consumer-reporting/measures/index.html.

Berwick, D., and D. Fox. 2016. "Evaluating the Quality of Medical Care: Donabedian's Classic Article 50 Years Later." *Milbank Quarterly: A Journal of Population Health and Health Policy* 94 (2): 237–41.

Centers for Medicare & Medicaid Services. 2020. "Quality Measures." Modified February 11. www.cms.gov/Medicare/Quality-Initiatives-Patient-Assessment-Instruments/QualityMeasures.

National Committee for Quality Assurance. 2021. "HEDIS and Performance Measurement." Accessed August 31. www.ncqa.org/hedis/.

US Department of Veterans Affairs. 2020. "VHA Pain Management: Opioid Safety— Other Resources." Updated July 22. www.va.gov/PAINMANAGEMENT/Opioid_ Safety/Other_Resources.asp.

CHAPTER 9

How to Select and Manage the Best Key Performance Indicators for Your Organization

CHAPTER 8 DISCUSSED various key performance indicators (KPIs) and what healthcare organizations should do to implement them successfully. This chapter will guide organizations in choosing the right KPIs to help them achieve their vision.

KPIs can be established easily in the hospital setting because the most frequently used KPIs are those related to length of hospital stay, emergency room wait times, and hospital readmission rates. That said, KPIs can also be smoothly adopted in the primary care setting.

Before selecting the most fitting KPIs, an organization must identify its stakeholders, mission, and goals. Once these are established, the organization can use a KPI determination worksheet to choose which KPIs align with its objectives.

STAKEHOLDERS

The process starts when the organization identifies its stakeholders, who can include the following:

- **Board members:** The organization's governing body is the highest level responsible for the quality of care provided. It assumes responsibility for the oversight of such items as quality initiatives, cost control, and patient experience.
- **Patients and families:** In the environment of the patient-centered medical home (PCMH; see more on this topic in chapters 2 and 3), the patient and family are the focus of performance initiatives aimed at improving quality, safety, and patient experience. Because the relationship between the organization and patient is becoming more complex, patients and their

families have grown increasingly involved at the developmental and planning stages of improvement initiatives.

- **Staff:** As the implementers of change, staff play a vital role in performance indicators as they are carrying out the tasks needed to reach the organization's goals. Thus, staff engagement is critical to achieving KPIs. The organization must provide the coaching and tools needed to make staff successful in their efforts.
- **Providers:** As the key players in ensuring patients receive good healthcare, providers are obliged to deliver high-quality care while maintaining patient safety.
- **Insurance companies:** Many patients and employers purchase their healthcare plans directly from insurance companies. Both parties need to balance cost with services provided.
- **Policymakers:** They work to create the framework in which healthcare is delivered.

Once the stakeholders have been determined, the next items to establish are the mission and objectives.

MISSION

The intent of a mission statement is to formally establish an organization's purpose: how it sees itself and wants to be perceived. The statement should concisely communicate the reason for the organization's existence:

- "We envision . . ."
- "To be the . . ."
- "We hope to . . ."

Mission statements point the organization in the direction it wants to go. They help to set a strategic plan for guiding decision making, aimed at achieving a set of goals within an established time frame.

OBJECTIVES

The next step is to create objectives: concise actions or steps that the organization must implement to move closer to reaching its goals and desired state. Objectives should be precise, measurable, and achievable on a set time frame. The following are examples of healthcare objectives:

- **Quality objective:** To improve blood pressure control rates through more nurse follow-up visits over the next six months.

- **Safety objective:** To decrease adverse events caused by medication errors over the next fiscal year.
- **Patient experience objective:** To improve patient experience by reducing wait times.

After setting objectives, the organization can move to selecting the KPIs that will facilitate its mission.

GOALS

In Chapter 3, we explained the benefits of SMART goals to patient outcomes; however, organizations can use this goal-setting process to select KPIs. Because the number of performance measures is overwhelming, applying the acronym SMART (specific, measurable, attainable, realistic, and timely) to the various KPIs can help the organization drill down to those that will align with the mission and get the organization to its desired state.

Exhibit 9.1 describes how to use SMART goals when choosing a KPI.

Meaningful is not part of the SMART goals acronym, but it should be added when choosing KPIs, as it is likely the most significant factor in the selection process.

Meaningful KPIs

KPIs will have different meanings to different healthcare organizations. Selecting meaningful performance measures ensures information will be created and shared for the purposes of improving patient care. Data should be meaningfully used to improve quality of care, patient safety, and staff efficiency. Metrics should be relevant to the stakeholders with the goal of significantly improving outcomes.

Exhibit 9.1: Using SMART Goals to Choose Key Performance Indicators

Specific	Is it specific enough to attain real data?
Measurable and meaningful	Is it measurable, trackable, and quantifiable? Does it have a significant impact on any stakeholders?
Attainable	Is it challenging but possible?
Realistic	Is it achievable by the organization? If change is required, are the organization and staff able to implement the change?
Timely	Is the KPI attainable over a predetermined period?

Selecting meaningful KPIs is a critical step. The organization must thoughtfully evaluate and select metrics that are purposeful, impactful, and relevant to the stakeholders. This process requires careful consideration as it will be the key factor in motivating the implementation process. See appendix K for a SMART KPI worksheet to help the organization work through selecting meaningful KPIs.

How to Evaluate and Select Meaningful Quality Measures

Exhibit 8.2 in chapter 8 lists several examples of HEDIS (Healthcare Effectiveness Data and Information Set) KPIs, but it is not exhaustive. There are many more to select from, which can become overwhelming for an organization. The Agency for Healthcare Research and Quality (AHRQ 2008) published a report titled "Identifying, Categorizing, and Evaluating Health Care Efficiency Measures" that provides guidance on how to properly vet each KPI for appropriateness and meaningfulness to the organization. Exhibit 9.2 lists the characteristics AHRQ recommends for assessing performance measures.

Once meaningful KPIs are selected, the organization must make sure quality data are available to be collected and turned into useful information. Data are simply a collection of numbers, facts, and statistics; information is created when data become significant and can be translated into useful results.

Defining Quality Data

Quality data refers to data that can be analyzed and used for their intended purpose. Organizations require quality data to give them insight into their current

---

Exhibit 9.2: AHRQ Recommended Characteristics

Important	Is the measure assessing an aspect of efficiency that is important to providers, payers, and policymakers? Has the measure been applied at the level of interest to those planning to use the measure? Is there an opportunity for improvement? Is the measure under the control of the provider or health system?
Scientifically sound	Can the measure be assessed reliably and reproducibly? Does the measure appear to capture the concept of interest? Is there evidence of construct or predictive validity?
Feasible	Are the data necessary to construct the measure available? Is the cost and burden of measurement reasonable?
Actionable	Are the results interpretable? Can the intended audience use the information to make decisions or take action?

Source: Data from Agency for Healthcare Research and Quality (2008).

Exhibit 9.3: AHIMA Characteristics

Accessibility	Data are attainable and available.
Consistency	Data are reliable and easily duplicated in the same setting under the same circumstances.
Currency	Data are current and up to date.
Granularity	Data are detailed.
Precision	Data are precise with minimal variability.
Accuracy	Data are correct and valid.
Comprehensiveness	Data are exhaustive and include all required elements.
Definition	Data definitions are clear and understood by all users.
Relevancy	Data are meaningful to those who analyze them and those they affect.
Timeliness	Data are available in real time.

Source: Data from Davoudi et al. (2015).

state and guide decision making. The American Health Information Management Association created a list of characteristics to help better understand what constitutes high-quality data (Davoudi 2015). Exhibit 9.3 lists the characteristics identified by the AHIMA Data Quality Management Model. These criteria can be used to vet data to ensure they meet the organization's standards for its selected KPI.

Additional Considerations

Consider these factors when selecting KPIs that will help set the organization up for success.

Choose Well-Established KPIs

There is a benefit to selecting existing and well-tested metrics. Chapter 8 noted the overlap of quality measures between the Centers for Medicare & Medicaid's Core Measures and the National Committee for Quality Assurance's HEDIS. Although many other KPIs exist, these agencies have provided evidence to support the value of their metrics.

Consider the Impact

Choose KPIs that will greatly benefit either a high volume of patients or high-risk patients. Also, consider their potential for increasing staff workload. To win staff buy-in, they must see the outcome of KPIs as worthwhile.

Resist Selecting Too Many KPIs

At first the organization may be tempted to focus on multiple KPIs. The task of tracking KPIs and developing performance improvement activities can be daunting. Also, getting buy-in from staff to focus on several metrics at once may be difficult. It is best to limit the number of performance measures to those that are most meaningful and will have significant outcomes.

YOU SELECTED YOUR KPI, NOW WHAT?

Now that you have selected the KPIs that will help get your organization to its desired state, we will review an example of what is needed to successfully realize the goal.

The Implementation Phase

Exhibit 9.4 shows how the PCMH can help with implementing a KPI.

Exhibit 9.4: KPI Implementation Example

KPI Selected: HEDIS Cardiovascular Conditions

Metric: Controlling blood pressure

Data Needed: Total number of patients with a diagnosis of high blood pressure

Heath Information System: The data system must be able to compile accurately and reliably both the total number of patients with an appropriate diagnosis reflecting high blood pressure and the total number of patients with well-controlled blood pressure. Ideally this is given as a percentage. An outlier report should be provided so that the primary care team can target outlier patients who need closer monitoring and interventions. This is a vital component for the team to be able to improve their individual scores. Monthly scorecards provide awareness (see chapter 5 for more information on scorecards).

Performance Improvement Activities:
1. Bring awareness of blood pressure control rates through provider scorecards.
2. Coach providers on proper diagnosis and treatment.
3. Educate providers on how to access their patient panel reports with outlier patients.

Monitoring: Give the primary care team monthly data to track their performance and provide frequent communication of their patient scores.

Using the PCMH: The patient-centered medical home ensures care is tailored to the patient. Under this model, a partnership between the patient and the primary care team facilitates high-quality outcomes. (See chapters 2 and 3 for more information on the PCMH and

(continued)

Exhibit 9.4: KPI Implementation Example (*continued*)

patient-centered goal setting.) The following are examples of how the PCMH can specifically aid in improving services to help attain high-quality outcomes for blood pressure:

- **Patient-centered care:** This model can be particularly useful for establishing blood pressure goals and defining how to realistically obtain these goals. The primary care team can also focus on a tailored plan for the patient, which can involve additional supporting team members depending on the patient's needs.
- **Coordinated care:** Having the pharmacist review medication to ensure it is appropriate can help confirm the right medication is being given to the right patient. A nutritionist can educate patients on a low-sodium diet to help them lower their blood pressure through dietary modifications.
- **Accessible services:** The registered nurse can bring the patient back for frequent blood pressure checks and medication adjustment until the patient reaches the blood pressure goal.
- **Comprehensive care:** Make sure the patient comprehends the implications of uncontrolled blood pressure by assessing the patient's health literacy to better tailor education and a treatment plan. (See chapter 2 for health literacy assessment tools)

The Monitoring Phase

Once the KPIs are selected and the process for performance improvement has been implemented, the organization should shift to a monitoring phase. During this time, evaluation and continuous reevaluation are important to make sure the KPIs remain meaningful and useful. Goals may need to be reset to confirm they are realistic. Data should be frequently compiled to guarantee reliability. Realistic time frames should also be considered and may need to be modified.

Sustaining Change

Stakeholders must consider sustainability at the beginning of the process improvement phase to make improved outcomes and processes the norm. To sustain change, a culture shift must be achieved through communication and engagement. Champions can help engage and excite the staff about process improvements. Committees can be formed to ensure change is maintained through the continuous monitoring of metrics. Management and leadership should keep the momentum going with constant communication through staff meetings, huddles, and visual management boards. Even when goals are reached, staff should be motivated to continue good performance and celebrated for maintaining their success. With these efforts in place, the organization can not only achieve the desired results but also maintain and build on them.

KEY POINTS

- The stakeholders, mission, and objectives must be established before choosing KPIs.
- A SMART KPI worksheet can be used to select KPIs.
- Meaningful KPIs are critical for buy-in and implementation of process improvement efforts.
- The AHIMA Data Quality Management Model can be used to assess high-quality data.
- The PCMH is well suited for process improvement efforts to reach KPI goals.
- Sustaining improvement outcomes requires a culture shift through communication and engagement.

REFERENCES

Agency for Healthcare Research and Quality. 2008. "Identifying, Categorizing, and Evaluating Health Care Efficiency Measures." Published April. https://archive.ahrq.gov/research/findings/final-reports/efficiency/efficiency.pdf.

Davoudi, S., J. Dooling, B. Glondys, T. Jones, L. Kadlec, S. M. Overgaard, K. Ruben, and A. Wendicke. 2015. "Data Quality Management Model (Updated)." *Journal of American Health Information Management Association* 86 (10): 62–65.

ADDITIONAL RESOURCES

Layman, E. 2009. "Research and Policy Model for Health Informatics and Information Management." *Perspectives in Health Information Management* 6 (Summer): 1g.

Silver, S., R. McQuillan, Z. Harel, A. Weizman, A. Thomas, G. Nesrallah, C. Bell, C. Chan, and G. Chertow. 2016. "How to Sustain Change and Support Continuous Quality Improvement." *Clinical Journal for the American Society of Nephrology* 11 (5): 916–24.

CHAPTER 10

The Last Word: Lessons from the Pandemic

COVID-19 HAS BEEN a catalyst for change across the entire healthcare landscape. Many of these changes are welcome and sustainable going forward. In the preceding chapters, we discussed the impact of the pandemic on specific aspects of primary care. Let's take it a step further as a way to summarize and build on that discussion with a few final thoughts.

> COVID-19 has been a catalyst for change across the entire healthcare landscape. Many of these changes are welcome and sustainable going forward.

What have we learned about ourselves, our staff, and our patients as we were forced to consider alternatives to the usual way of doing business? We discovered that we can be flexible, creative, adaptive, and resilient. We found new paths toward addressing the needs of our patients. But most of all, this pandemic experience has reinforced our belief that it's the people that matter. Indeed, they are the heart of healthcare.

Never has it been more important to address resilience on all fronts. Let's explore ways to continue the path forward, using the foundation we built during the pandemic.

BUILDING RESILIENCE

Gratitude can be a comfort during tough times. It was a popular theme through the pandemic, and it continues to be a particularly fitting topic to discuss with staff in this post-pandemic environment when helping them reflect, learn, and build resiliency.

The health effects of gratitude are significant. Oppland (2021) offers a list of benefits:

- Improves physical health
- Improves sleep
- Improves psychological health
- Increases empathy
- Reduces aggression
- Expands social connections
- Enhances self-esteem
- Improves mental strength

You don't need to look too far to find effective exercises to conduct with your staff. For instance, you could start a team meeting by asking, round robin style, the simple question, "What are you grateful for today?' As team members respond, a positive attitude builds—a great way to start the day!

You could also establish a "gratitude jar," and ask staff to write down something they are grateful for and put it in the jar. During a particularly stressful day, you can read submissions from the jar to give the staff a boost.

Also, as you round, make it a point to express gratitude to the staff, thanking them for their efforts. A simple thank you might be just what someone needs to get through a tough day.

Feel free to create your own approach; get staff involved. Homegrown activities will feel more meaningful to all parties and engender a sense of ownership.

SUSTAINING THE GAINS

Identify, discuss, and celebrate all the wonderful moments when staff stepped up during the pandemic to provide compassionate, personalized care to your patients in a time of uncertainty and unusual stress. When they look back and realize how they made a difference when put to the test, they'll know that they are capable of just about anything. Talk about how to use these gains to plan for the future of your practice or clinic. Shared stress and trauma, and getting through it successfully, can be galvanizing!

> Shared stress and trauma, and getting through it successfully, can be galvanizing!

And don't forget to include your patients in these discussions. After all, they went through it, too, and they can be a great source for identifying what went well and what needs improvement.

SELF-CARE

Key to achieving personal mastery—a core competency for leaders—is an intentional focus on self-care. If you weren't doing this pre-pandemic, now is the time to build it into your daily routine. Exercise, meditation, adequate sleep, spending time with friends and family—these are all forms of self-care. The list goes on. Anthony Fauci, MD, stated in an interview during the American College of Healthcare Executives 2021 Congress on Healthcare Leadership that he "simply doesn't feel right " if he doesn't run three or four miles every day (Bowen, 2021).

> Key to achieving personal mastery—a core competency for leaders—is an intentional focus on self-care.

Role-model this behavior by creating a culture of wellness and provide opportunities for your staff to practice short moments of self-care. Look back to chapter 4 for ideas around staff wellness.

FLEXIBILITY AND ADAPTABILITY

Chapter 1 described flexibility and adaptability as core leadership competencies. These were certainly put to the test during the pandemic. We all learned to "pivot." Think about the practices and procedures that you "flexed" and "adapted" to make things work: telehealth, flexible schedules, remote working. Which of those approaches are viable going forward? Focus deeply on the moments that matter to both your patients and your staff, and hardwire the most valued adaptations.

Last, as Napoleon Bonaparte proclaimed, "A leader is a dealer in hope." Before, during, and after a crisis, such as the COVID-19 pandemic, the leader's role is to communicate clearly and often while connecting staff to purpose. Describe to staff what success looks like and what is possible, then help them get there. We hope that this book has given you some tools to begin that journey.

KEY POINTS

- COVID-19 has been a catalyst for change across the entire healthcare landscape.
- The health effects of gratitude are significant.
- Shared stress and trauma, and getting through them successfully, can be galvanizing!
- Key to achieving personal mastery—a core competency for leaders—is an intentional focus on self-care.

- Focus deeply on the moments that matter to both your patients and your staff, and hardwire the most valued adaptations.

REFERENCES

Bowen, D. 2021. "Cultivating Resilience." *Healthcare Executive*. Published May/June. www.ache.org/blog/2021/cultivating-resilience.

Oppland, M. 2021. "13 Most Popular Gratitude Exercises & Activities." Published July 2. https://positivepsychology.com/gratitude-exercises/.

SMART Goals Worksheet for Diabetes

SMART goals are: Specific, Measurable, Attainable, Realistic, Timely

Patients who choose their own goals, with the support of their primary care team, do better with long-term disease management.

What is one thing you would like to do to improve your diabetes? Here are some examples:

Count carbohydrates   Check your blood sugar   Take your medication

Exercise   Weight reduction   Check your feet daily

WHAT will you do? _____   **WHEN** will you do it? _____
HOW will you do it? _____   **WHERE** will you do it? _____

On a scale of 1–10, how important is this goal to you? _____
How confident are you that you will achieve your goal? _____

Things that can make it difficult to achieve your goal: _____

_____

The plan for overcoming these difficulties: _____

_____

How can your primary care team help? _____

_____

Studies show that patients who control their diabetes with an HbA1c of 7 percent or less live longer, healthier lives with fewer complications. Don't wait; take control of your diabetes today.

Source: Adapted from Jordan, L. 2017. "Health Literacy, Self-Management Goals Made Simple." Presentation at The Joint Commission Conference, April 6.

Appointment Prep Checklist

Appointment Prep Checklist for Patient:	Y	N	N/A
Concern:			
Concern:			
Concern:			
1. Are needed labs/imaging complete with a copy in the chart?			
2. Obtained needed forms?			
3. Obtained hospital discharge records?			
4. Updated list of patient medication?			
5. Insurance information obtained?			
6. Is patient getting the preferred appointment type (telephone, video, face to face)?			
7. Updated blood pressure/blood sugar log in chart?			

Shared Medical Appointment: Diabetes

Target Audience: 4–5 patients with diabetes

Facilitator: Physician, Nurse Practitioner, Physician Assistant

Support Staff: Nurse, Nutritionist, Pharmacist

Appointment Guide:

8:00–8:30	**Patient arrival check-in**
	Nurse:
	   Consent forms signed
	   Obtain vital signs and blood sugar logs

8:30–9:30	**Facilitator:**
	   Welcome patients
	   Education on fasting and postprandial blood sugar goals
	   Review of individual blood sugar logs
	   Medication adjustments

9:30–10:00	**Pharmacist:**
	   Review of medication
	   Assess for possible interactions
	   Discuss how to properly take medication
	   Ensure all medication and supplies are up to date

10:00–10:30	**Nutritionist:**
	   Review of carbohydrates
	   Establish goal for carbohydrates per meal

10:30–11:00	**Nurse:**
	Additional education tailored to patients
	How to properly administer insulin injections
	Rule of 15 for hypoglycemic episodes
	Refer to specialists for additional interventions (e.g., podiatry, optometry)
	Ensure patient is scheduled for next shared medical appointment and any needed labs

Shared Medical Appointment
Preparation Checklist

Completed By: Nurse _____ **Date** _____

Patient Name	Medication	CV Disease Yes/No	A1c	GFR	Micro-albumin	Eye Exam	Foot Exam

This checklist will allow the provider to navigate through the shared medical appointment seamlessly. All data required for medical decision making and medication changes are collated and made readily available on this checklist.

Process Improvement Poster Template

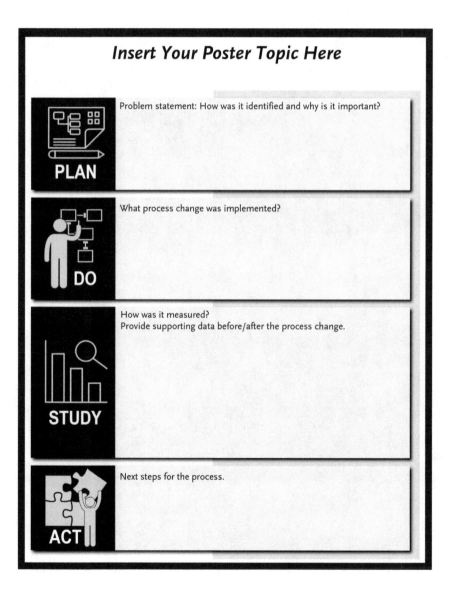

Leader Rounding Tool

Clinic: _____ Date: _____ Person conducting rounds: _____

Before rounding:

- Coordinate with the clinic/unit supervisor. This is a collaborative effort, not a sneak attack.
- Make sure follow-up items from previous rounds have been resolved.

Questions for leaders to ask staff:

What things are going well in the clinic?	Notes:
What are you most proud of?	
What is frustrating you with the work?	Notes:
What barriers/issues get in the way of you doing your best work?	
How should they be addressed?	
Do you have the	Notes:
resources/tools/equipment that you need?	
What feedback, if any, have you heard from patients and families about their experience at the clinic?	Notes:
What else would you like leadership to know?	Notes:

Summarize notes from conversations you had with patients or families:

After rounds:

- Set priorities for problem solving based on information gathered and issues identified.
- Include supervisors and staff in process improvements.
- Close the loop. Let staff know how their issue was resolved and thank them for identifying the opportunity for improvement.
- Celebrate success!

APPENDIX G

Personal Development Plan Template

The **goals** of a personal development plan (PDP) are things you want to achieve to improve in your career. **Objectives** are meaningful steps toward goals, typically designed to be **SMART** (specific, measurable, achievable, realistic, and timely). Goals can be the higher-level items that aren't as measurable.

Long-Term Goals

Short-Term Goals

Goal	Objective	Resources Required	Activity	Target Date/ Status

Patient/Family Advisory Council
Sample Charter

Purpose: The patient/family advisory council (PFAC) will have an active role in improving the patient and family experience at the Clinic, serving as a voice for patients and family members through input and feedback into programs, processes, and environmental design.

PFAC PATIENT AND FAMILY MEMBER RESPONSIBILITIES

- Complete an application and interview prior to selection
- Sign a confidentiality statement
- Actively participate in council meetings, prepared for each session
- Effectively collaborate with a diverse membership
- Represent patients and their families to ensure the best possible patient and family experience at the clinic
- Serve for a term of two years, with the option to renew for a second term
- Support decisions that are made by consensus
- Adhere to the organization's Code of Conduct

ROLES

- Co-chairs: Patient advocate and a patient/family advisor
- Clinic members: Supervisor, one provider, one nurse, one medical service assistant
- Patient/family advisors: Four clinic patients, two family members
- Community representative

PROCEDURES

- The PFAC will develop annual goals at the beginning of the calendar year.
- All members will have voting privileges.
- If consensus is not reached, decisions will be made by a majority vote.
- An annual report on the effectiveness of the PFAC will be prepared at the end of the calendar year.

MEETINGS

- Meetings will be held monthly on each first Tuesday between 5 p.m. and 7 p.m.
- Agendas will be developed by the co-chairs.
- Minutes will be distributed within one week of a meeting. A scribe will be appointed from the Clinic member group.

Note: See the references at the end of chapter 6 for more details to customize your PFAC charter.

Onstage–Offstage Design

The schematic on the following page shows a sample onstage–offstage design.

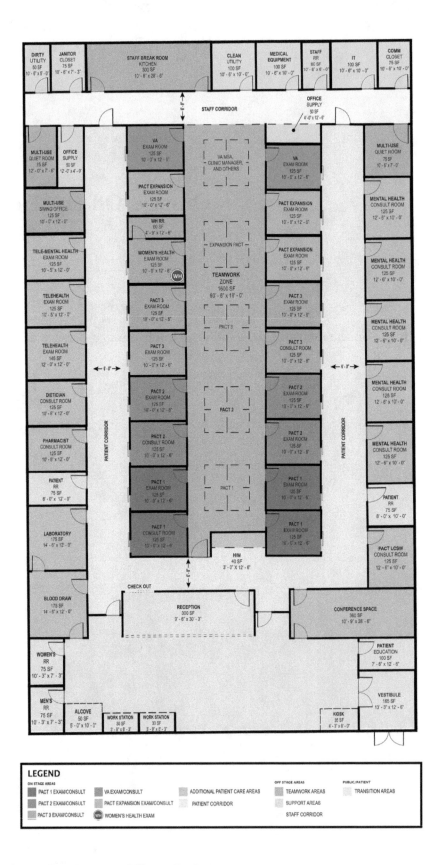

Mystery Shopping List

Clinic: _____ Date: _____ Shopper: _____

Instructions: Accompany a patient who has an appointment at the clinic. You are undercover as a relative or friend.

Note: Some questions require a yes/no answer, others a rating.

Arrival at the Facility

Question	Yes/No	Rating: 1 (very poor)–5 (excellent)	Comments
How visible and clear was exterior signage?			
Was parking available when you arrived and close to the clinic?			
Was accessible parking available when you arrived?			
Was there a covered drop-off area at the entrance?			
Rate the exterior of the building and the grounds.			
Rate access for people with disabilities.			
Rate interior signage directing you to the clinic.			

Check-In at the Clinic

Question	Yes/No	Rating: 1 (very poor)–5 (excellent)	Comments
Did the receptionist greet the patient warmly, making eye contact?			
Was the receptionist's name tag visible?			
Rate the receptionist on courtesy, respect, and maintaining patient privacy.			
How would the patient rate their check-in experience?			
Rate the waiting room experience re: healing environment, waiting time.			

Clinical Encounter: Rooming

Question	Yes/No	Rating: 1 (very poor)–5 (excellent)	Comments
Did the nurse summon patient by first name only?			
Did the nurse provide a warm greeting, making eye contact, and introducing themself?			
Did the nurse treat the patient with courtesy and respect, explaining what was going to happen during the visit?			
Did the nurse protect the patient's privacy?			
How well did the nurse listen to the patient?			
How would the patient rate the experience?			

Clinical Encounter: Provider

Question	Yes/No	Rating: 1 (very poor)–5 (excellent)	Comments
Did the patient wait long in the exam room for the provider?			
Did the provider give a warm greeting, making eye contact, and introducing themself?			
Did the provider treat the patient with courtesy and respect, explaining what was going to happen during the visit?			
Did the provider protect the patient's privacy?			
How well did the provider listen to the patient?			
Did the provider include the patient in the treatment planning?			
Did the provider communicate in terms the patient could understand?			
How would the patient rate the experience?			

Checkout

Question	Yes/No	Rating: 1 (very poor)–5 (excellent)	Comments
Was the patient given clear instructions both orally and in writing?			
Was a follow-up appointment made, if needed?			
How would the patient rate the experience?			

Feel free to customize this shopping list to suit your needs by adding your own questions.

SMART KPI Worksheet

Organization: _____

Stakeholders: _____

Mission Statement: _____

Objectives: _____

_____

_____

_____

_____

_____

_____

_____

_____

KPI: _____

KPI: _____

KPI: _____

KPI: _____

KPI: _____

S SPECIFIC		
Criteria: Specific enough to attain real data.		
M MEASURABLE AND MEANINGFUL		
Criteria: Measurable, trackable, quantifiable, impactful.		
A ATTAINABLE		
Criteria: Challenging but possible.		
R REALISTIC		
Criteria: Achievable and able to implement change.		
T TIMELY		
Criteria: Attainable over a specific time frame.		

Index

Note: Italicized page locators refer to exhibits.

Behavioral healthcare specialists: virtual care and, 49

Behavioral health staff: supporting primary care team and, 29, 30, 31

Benchmarking: external, 130–31; internal, 131

Bernard J. Tyson National Award for Excellence in Pursuing Healthcare Equity, 7

Beryl Institute: Consumer Survey, 2, 3; patient experience as defined by, 1

Billing: surprise, 3

Blame: avoiding, 12

Blood pressure control: process for improving, 134, *134*

Board members: identifying, KPI selection and, 139

Bonaparte, Napoleon, 149

Bondura, K., 119

Bourne, D., 64

Brainstorming, 61

Bullying, 14

Bundled payments, 5

Burnout, 56, 57–58, 60, 87; cardinal symptoms of, 84; causes of, 83–84; decreased, patient-centered medical homes and, 8; "don't list" and, 85; interventions for, 84–85; provider, protecting against, 83–85. *See also* Resilience

Cancer Care Survey Measures (CAHPS), 132

Care coordination, 5

Career development opportunities, 70

Caregivers: list of functions provided by, 104; supporting, 104, *105,* 110

Caring: creating universal language of, 13

Case managers, 23

Cause-and-effect diagrams, 61

Centers for Disease Control and Prevention (CDC), 131

Centers for Medicare & Medicaid Services (CMS), 88, 134, 135, 136, 143; community health assessments required by, 93; Core Measures, categorization of, 124; Core Quality Measures Collaborative, 124; metrics as quality measures, *125*

Chain of command, 78

Champions: change management and roles/responsibilities of, *15*

Change: resistance to, 14

Change management, 14–16, 17, 78; getting ready for, 14–15; roles and responsibilities for, *15*; sponsors and, 14; sustaining change, 16; tools for, 15–16

Chart reviews, 129

Chief population health officer, 94

Chronic disease management: shared medical appointments and, 24

Chronic obstructive pulmonary disease: shared medical appointments and, 24

Chunk and Check, 100

Clinician and Group Survey Measures (CAHPS), 132

Clinic managers: rounding with, 67

Clinic Manager's Toolkit, 69

Clutter: reducing, 115, 121

Coaching: providers for leadership, 82

Codesign, 114

Color-coded signage, 116

Committees, 54; encouraging participation in, 81–82, 89; steering, 82–83

Communication breakdowns, 40–41

Community health assessments: creative healthcare solutions and, 93–94; parameters in, 93

Compassion, 12, 57–58, 71; definition of, 57; showing, 58

Compassion fatigue, 56, 84

Compensation: not equated with job satisfaction, 73–74

Competence: followers and, 12

Competencies: for successful transitions, 15–16; for transformational leaders, 10–11

Competition: for healthcare services, 1

Comprehensive care: as core element of PCMH, 19, 20–22, 32, 34; services offered under, 20, *21*; tailoring through assessment and care plans, 38–40, 50

Comprehensive care plan: formulating, 22; modified life cycle, 22, *22*

Hartford Foundation, 8

Healing arts, 116–17

Healing design, principles of, 112–17, 121; access and healing, design objectives for, 113; access to nature, 114–15; codesign, 114; decluttering, 115; efficiency, 114; healing arts, 116–17; patient experience, design objectives for, 112; quiet and privacy, 116; team-based care, design objectives for, 112–13; way-finding, 115–16

Health: WHO definition of, 96

Healthcare: Donabedian model for evaluating quality in, 49, 50, 132–33; relational nature of, 2, 3

Healthcare access. See Access

Healthcare costs: increases in, 5

Healthcare Effectiveness Data and Information Set (HEDIS), 3, 79, 134, 135, 136, 143; commonly used metrics., 126–27; diabetes scores, provider metrics for, 80, 80; key domains of care, 126; measures, practical application and additional benefits with, 128; measures, using, 126–28

Healthcare utilization: integrated primary care and rate of, 9

Health equity, 5–7; addressing, initiatives across the country, 6

Health literacy, 100–103, 109; addressing, tools and strategies for, 100; assessing, 22; definition of, 100; full disclosure and, 103; high-reliability organization framework for safety and, 103; patient education and, 101; patient/family advisory councils and, 101–3

Health Plan Survey Measures (CAHPS), 132

Health Resources & Services Administration: PCMH certification and recognition, 16

Heart failure: diagnosis-based shared medical appointment for, 45, 45; diet and, 30; shared medical appointments and management of, 24

HEDIS. See Healthcare Effectiveness Data and Information Set (HEDIS)

HHS. See US Department of Health and Human Services (HHS)

High-performing healthcare organizations: access and, 2

High-reliability organizations (HROs): safety forums in, 67–68; staff engagement and, 64–68, 71

Hippocratic Oath, 2

Honesty: followers and, 12

Hospital Compare ratings, 3

Huddles: sample agenda for, 65

Humility: transformational leaders and, 10, 11

Hypertension: drop-in shared medical appointment for, 45, 46; shared medical appointments and management of, 24

"Identifying, Categorizing, and Evaluating Health Care Efficiency Measures" (AHRQ), 142

IHI. See Institute for Healthcare Improvement (IHI)

Incentives: rewards and, 62; for using patient-centered medical homes, 8

Inclusion officers positions, creating, 6

Inclusive environment: equitable access and, 6

Information: enhancing access to, 106–7, 110

Information systems, strong: benchmarking and, 130–31; checklist, 130; data triggers as critical in, 129–30; investing in, 129–31

Institute for Healthcare Improvement (IHI), 4, 9, 23, 58; health equity framework and self-assessment tool, 6–7

Insurance companies: identifying, KPI selection and, 140

Integrated primary care: impact of, on specific aspects of care, 9

Integrity, 11, 14

Intermountain Healthcare, 9

Interpersonal effectiveness: transformational leaders and, 10–11

Interviews, 54, 128

Januvia, 39, 40, 41

Job satisfaction: compensation not equated with, 73–74; quality improvement and, 86–88

Sponsors: change management and, 14

Staff: growth and development, 68–69, 71; healing environment for, 118–19; identifying, KPI selection and, 140; involvement with metrics, encouraging, 133–36; meaningful recognition of, 61–62; wellness programs for, 57. *See also* Providers; Supporting primary care team

Staff engagement, 53–71; burnout and resilience, 57–58; caring culture and, 12; connecting to purpose, 55–56; customer experience standards and, 55; employee experience and, 70; good leadership, 54; high-reliability organizations and, 64–68, 71; impact of the "why?" and, 56–57, 71; joy in the workplace, 58; levels of, *59*, 59–64; measuring of quality and safety and, 50; onboarding, importance of, 54; personal healthcare experiences illustrative of, 53, 70–71; staff growth and development, 68–69; supporting the managers, 69–70

Staff meetings: sample agenda for, 66

Stakeholders: staff as, 133

Standard deviations: variability of data and, 129

State of Healthcare Quality Report: HEDIS and data provision through, 128

Steering committees, 82

Stewardship: organizational, transformational leaders and, 10

"Stopping the line," safety and, 64

Stories: knowing, patient engagement and, 96–97, 98; sharing, 13, 56, 57, 103

Storming stage: in Tuckman model, 82

Stress: burnout and, 83; trauma and, shared during pandemic, 148, 149

Structure: in Donabedian model, *50*, 132

Success: celebrating, awareness, 15

Supervisors: change management and roles/ responsibilities of, *15*

Supporting primary care team, 29–31; behavioral health staff, 29, 30, 31; medical assistant, 29, 31; nurse educator, 29, 30; nutritionist, 29, 30; pharmacist, 29, 30, 31; social worker, 29, 30–31. *See also* Primary care team; Providers; Staff

Surgical Care Survey Measures (CAHPS), 132

Surprise billing, 3

Surveys, 10, 120, 121, 128, 131, 132

Systems thinking, 10, 14

Teach-back, 100

Team-based care: design objectives for, 112–13

Teams: examining employee engagement, 61–62, *62*; multidisciplinary, 24, 27, 32; PCMH, 27–28; primary care, assembling for PCMH, 33

Technical competencies: transformational leaders and, 10

Technology: patient access and role of, 107–8, 110

Telehealth, 5, 17, 106, 107, 111, 149; service examples, *108*; telemedicine *vs.*, 44; when to use, 43

Telemedicine, 32, 107; appointments, 23; challenges related to, 49; COVID-19 and, 48; telehealth *vs.*, 44; when to use, 43

Telephone appointments, 23

Text-messaging services, 108

Therapy dog visits, 117

Timeliness/timely care, 2; healthcare quality and, 26; performance improvement (PI) initiatives and, *26*

Time pressures: burnout and, 83–84

Training: change management and, 16

Transformational leaders: caring culture and, 12–14

Transformational leadership: attributes of, 9; competencies for, 10–11

Translation services, 100

Transparency, 67, 103, 107

Trust, 2, 14

Trzeciak, S., 57

Tuckman model: five stages of development in, 82

Tyson, Bernard J., 7

About the Authors

Mary-Ellen Piche, LFACHE, CPHQ, is a consultant who provides services to healthcare and nonprofit organizations in strategic planning, organizational assessment and development, patient experience improvement, leadership development and coaching, high reliability, and quality management and accreditation. She is a faculty associate of the American College of Healthcare Executives (ACHE).

Piche's expertise in healthcare quality, patient experience, leadership, and high reliability is based on more than 40 years' experience in clinical, leadership, teaching, and consultant roles that have taken her across the United States and abroad.

Piche holds a baccalaureate degree in applied science and technology from Thomas Edison State University and board certifications in healthcare quality and healthcare management. She is a Life Fellow of ACHE.

Piche serves on the board of directors of Rockefeller College's Center for Women in Government and Civil Society, where she gives frequent presentations to the fellows in the public policy and new leaders programs. She also serves on the boards of directors of WMHT (the regional PBS station) and Trinity Health St. Peter's ambulatory surgery center.

Gina Luna FNP-BC, BC-ADM, has been in the healthcare field for more than 15 years. She has worked in clinical practice as a registered nurse and nurse practitioner and has transitioned to quality management. She is now the chief quality manager for an organization with more than 20 clinics.

Luna obtained her bachelor of science degree in biology from Loyola Marymount University. Knowing she wanted to work in healthcare, she went on to earn bachelor of science and then master of science degrees in nursing from the University of Rochester. She is a board-certified family nurse practitioner and holds an additional board certification in advanced diabetes management.

Having worked in clinical and administrative settings, Luna brings the unique perspective of both points of view. As a clinician, she successfully deployed shared medical appointments and created tools to help nurse and provider efficiency. While working in quality management, she established an infection control program and multiple clinical performance committees, and successfully headed various performance-improvement activities.

Luna has also worked as a legal nurse consultant and diabetes consultant, developed webinars for ACHE, founded the local nurse practitioner chapter for the California Association for Nurse Practitioners, and served as assistant clinical professor for the University of California Los Angeles nursing program.